Jackie

Hope you enjoy!

John Grisham

CHEF *in the* VINEYARD

FRESH & SIMPLE RECIPES
FROM GREAT WINE ESTATES

JOHN SARICH

SEA·HILL
PRESS

Publisher's Acknowledgments

We would like to thank the many people involved
during the development of a book of this nature.
We would especially like to acknowledge the staff and
managers from all the wineries included in this book.

Debra McCloskey, Art Director,
Graphic and Promotional Services at Ste. Michelle Wine Estates,
for her input, art direction, and patience.
Ted Baseler, Kari Leitch, and Martin Johnson
for their support in the development of this book.

Published in the United States of America by
Sea-Hill Press, Inc.
P. O. Box 60301, Santa Barbara, CA 93160
www.seahillpress.com

Publisher: Greg Sharp
Art Director: Barbara Schmitt
Layout: Judy Petry
Editor: Cynthia Sharp
Winery Project Manager: Donna Duncanson

10 9 8 7 6 5 4 3 2 1
Printed in Hong Kong

CHEF *in the* VINEYARD

FRESH & SIMPLE RECIPES
FROM GREAT WINE ESTATES

JOHN SARICH

Author's Dedication

Saying thanks is not enough for some of the people who

have helped me in my culinary journey.

To Sheridan Merriex, who for years made sure I knew

I was going to Tokyo, not Toledo.

To the best culinary team in the wine business:

Janet, Kurt, Scott, Kim, and Regina.

Chef Kim Wiss of Antica Napa Valley for her expertise with menus and recipes.

To Greg Sharp, my publisher, for his patience and perseverance.

To my boys, Biagio and Dominic, for whom I continually strive

not to make just happy bellies, but happy hearts.

....

Photography

Kevin Cruff, Location Photography
Based in Seattle, Washington, Kevin Cruff specializes in location photography for diverse advertising and corporate clients such as Ste. Michelle Wine Estates, Amtrak, The Boeing Company, Chevrolet, and Nordstrom, Inc. His work has won recognition from prestigious trade publications that include *Communication Arts, AR100, Graphis, Print Magazine,* and *Photo District News.*
www.cruffphoto.com

Christopher Conrad, Cover Author Portrait
Christopher Conrad has been creating images for over twenty-five years.
His studio, Conrad & Company Photography, is located in Seattle, Washington.
www.conradfoto.com

Lindsey Eltinge, Food Photography
Lindsay has had a love of photography since she was a teenager. She specializes in food photography. Lindsey's studio is based in Santa Barbara, California.
www.lindseyeltinge.com

Charles Blackburn, www.blackburnpictures.com

Angie Norwood Brown, www.anbphoto.com

Della Chen, www.dellachen.com

Jennifer Hutter, Photograph, page 23, page 164
www.jenniferhutter.com

John Sarich, Food Styling

CONTENTS

ANATOMY OF A GREAT WINE ESTATE

By Ted Baseler
Ste. Michelle Wine Estates, President and CEO

I have been fortunate to have visited some of the most famous wine estates in the world. In spite of differences driven by geography, climate, culture, and conventions, there are things I always find the great wine estates have in common, beyond an unwavering commitment to quality. First, they have exceptional vineyards, and exceptional vineyards are born from a profound understanding of the delicate relationship between the land and the grapes.

Whether they have fifteen or three hundred years under their belts, the great wine estates know which grapes will thrive in their unique conditions on their spot of land—acre by acre and often row by row. Great wines reflect the place where they are grown.

Second, the great estates are innovators. This means doing things that have not been done before. It may mean defying convention or planting grapes where prevailing thought says you cannot. Without such trailblazers, today we would not have the wonderful "Super-Tuscans" spurred on by innovators like Piero Antinori. And it's hard to imagine the American wine landscape without the contributions of Napa Valley pioneer Warren Winiarski or Oregon's Dick Erath.

Third, the great wine estates have a memorable story to tell. They have learned that their wines are only as good as the total experience in which they are wrapped. Their stories involve the land, the region, cuisine, and local ingredients. The great wine estates tell their stories in the context of wine and food.

Chefs have become important storytellers. I knew when I first met John Sarich in the mid-1980s, that he had the passion for wine and food and the understanding of land and culture to become a great storyteller for our flagship wine estate, Chateau Ste. Michelle. In fact, I knew that John's culinary insight and expertise would be integral to our growth.

Our company started with a single pearl, Chateau Ste. Michelle. John Sarich helped add luster to it. Today we have a "string of pearls," a collection of estate wineries whose vineyards produce some of the best wines in the world. With John's help, we have built a culinary program that is unrivaled in the industry. He has a keen understanding of how flavors work together. His insight about wine and food is a reflection of his vast experiences with people and places.

John's ability to showcase great wines through stories of their region, cuisine, and food is a great gift. There is no tour guide I would rather follow through the world of wine and food than John Sarich. Enjoy!

FOOD AND WINE

By John Sarich

O NE DAY WHILE DRIVING in the countryside just east of Seattle, I passed a beautiful estate. I could tell something was happening and I was curious. The date was September 16, 1976, the day the new Chateau Ste. Michelle winery opened in Woodinville, Washington. I was aware of Ste. Michelle wines, but had not realized Ste. Michelle was opening a new winery. It was a day that changed my life.

When I took the tour that day, it struck me that I knew enough about wine (my family used to make their own) to give these tours. I was hired as a tour guide, intending just to make some money while I was in graduate school. Since I also loved to cook, I started cooking for winery guests and teaching cooking classes in the historic Manor House. I had found my passion, and I stayed.

I left school and headed to San Francisco to sell Chateau Ste. Michelle wines in California. Selling Washington wines in Napa's backyard was a challenge at that time. Quickly, I learned the value of putting the wine into the context of the land and the local food produced in the region. People were fascinated to learn about Chateau Ste. Michelle wines while sampling Northwest foods.

Eventually my passion for Northwest food and wine led me back to Seattle to pursue my dream of running my own restaurants. From 1980 to 1990 I was a head chef and owned two restaurants. But I was

never far from Chateau Ste. Michelle. In 1990, I returned to the winery to become Culinary Director. In that role, my travels have taken me around the world to cook with, and cook for, many famous people. But what truly makes me proud is having helped open the world's eyes to the quality wines being produced in the Pacific Northwest and California today.

In this book I will introduce you to ten great wine estates I have come to know and highly regard from Washington, Oregon, and California. Each wine estate features a menu, with local ingredients, that captures the essence of the region. You'll also find signature wines from the estate paired with each course. Throughout the book we have given suggestions for food and wine pairings, but the enjoyment of wine is often in the discovery. Sometimes the greatest rewards come from taking a leap of faith and trying something unexpected.

Wine Pairing

Food and wine are natural companions; one will make the other taste better. Making the perfect match can be as involved as you want to make it.

There is, at times, a physiological element to the match. For example, take the combination of raw oysters served with a beautiful oaky Napa Chardonnay. Together, these make a terrible match. The mineralogy and salty quality of the oysters will make the vanilla and butterscotch flavors of the wine taste just like wood. On the other hand, a non-oaked Chardonnay would be a wonderful pairing. When I travel, I always discover a new match that I wouldn't think would work, but turns out to be delicious. Do not be reluctant to be adventurous and to try new combinations.

This advice is especially true in a world with multi-cultural cuisines. It is not so much the salmon you are going to match the wine to, but what ingredients, style, and flavors make up that salmon recipe. Seared salmon with a wild-mushroom cream sauce would be perfect for that oaky Chardonnay. However, for a salmon teriyaki tartare the perfect match would be Riesling.

One easy way to think of matching food and wine is "bold flavored foods, bold flavored wines; delicate flavored foods, delicate flavored wines." This way one will not overpower the other. Always keep in mind that the bottom line is your enjoyment. If Merlot is the wine you like, by all means enjoy it with any meal.

Wine is a beverage best enjoyed with friends, family, and food. And that is a match that cannot be beat.

CHATEAU STE. MICHELLE is a popular destination for learning about wine and food. From impromtu picnics on the beautiful grounds, to food and wine classes taught in the historic Manor House, to multi-course gourmet dinners prepared by the winery's culinary team—there are many ways to enjoy learning about wine through the complement of food.

THESE FRESHLY HARVESTED *Cabernet Sauvignon grapes may ultimately find their way to the table as a wine to be enjoyed with full-flavored appetizers, a hearty beef dish, or even grilled salmon. Exploring the range of possibilities of food and wine pairings is half the enjoyment of wine.*

Guide to Food and Wine Pairing

	WHITE WINES				
	Riesling	Chenin Blanc	Gewürztraminer	Pinot Gris/Pinot Grigio	Semillon
	MEDIUM DRY	MEDIUM DRY	DRY	DRY	DRY
Mild Cheeses	🍃	🍃	🍃	🍃	🍃
Strongly Flavored Cheeses			🍃		
Appetizers	🍃	🍃	🍃	🍃	🍃
Oysters				🍃	🍃
Shrimp, Crab, and Lobster	🍃	🍃		🍃	
Clams and Mussels				🍃	🍃
Seafood with Wine or Light Sauces	🍃	🍃		🍃	🍃
Seafood with Cream Sauces				🍃	
Grilled Fish				🍃	
Salmon				🍃	
Cream Sauces				🍃	🍃
Mediterranean-Style Pasta					
Chicken, Turkey, and Game Hen	🍃	🍃	🍃	🍃	
Pheasant, Duck, and Goose			🍃		
Asian Cuisine	🍃	🍃	🍃	🍃	🍃
Pork and Veal			🍃		
Lamb					
Game					
Beef					
Fruit and Light Desserts					
Chocolate Desserts					

WHITE WINES				RED WINES						DESSERT WINES		
Sauvignon Blanc	Sparkling Wine or Champagne	Chardonnay	Non-Oak Chardonnay	Syrah/Shiraz	Pinot Noir	Zinfandel	Cabernet Franc	Merlot/Meritage	Cabernet Sauvignon	Late Harvest White Riesling	Late Harvest Semillon	Port
DRY				MEDIUM BODIED		FULL BODIED				SWEET		
🍃	🍃		🍃	🍃		🍃	🍃	🍃	🍃			
🍃	🍃	🍃		🍃		🍃	🍃	🍃	🍃	🍃	🍃	🍃
🍃			🍃									
🍃	🍃		🍃									
🍃		🍃	🍃									
🍃			🍃									
🍃		🍃	🍃									
	🍃											
🍃	🍃	🍃	🍃	🍃	🍃	🍃		🍃				
🍃	🍃	🍃		🍃	🍃	🍃		🍃				
🍃	🍃		🍃									
	🍃			🍃	🍃	🍃	🍃	🍃	🍃			
		🍃		🍃		🍃	🍃					
						🍃	🍃	🍃				
						🍃	🍃					
				🍃	🍃				🍃			
							🍃		🍃			
				🍃	🍃	🍃		🍃	🍃			
						🍃		🍃				
	🍃									🍃	🍃	🍃
							🍃		🍃			

The Pacific Northwest

THE PACIFIC NORTHWEST is distinguished by diverse and dramatic landscapes, violent geologic history, and a distinct seasonal climate, all which contribute to cultivating great grapes and an ever-increasing reputation as a world-class wine-growing region. Northerly latitude, climate, soil, geological foundation—these characteristics make Washington's Columbia Valley and Oregon's Willamette Valley the centerpiece of Northwest viticulture.

The unique vineyard locations of this region—sharing a latitude with France and longitude with California—truly blend to create a synthesis of Old World elegance and New World style. Washington State's primary wine region, the Columbia Valley, lies on the eastside of the Cascade Mountains. Here the landscape and weather are decidedly different from Seattle. The mountains shield the rain, limiting annual rainfall to six- to eight-inches. The skies are sunny, the climate is dry, and the soil is sparse—perfect conditions for growing world-class wine grapes.

The Willamette Valley of Oregon is the primary wine-growing region in that state. Unlike Washington, where vineyards thrive in the warm, dry conditions east of the Cascade Mountains, Oregon's vineyards have successfully optimized the cooler climate, marine influence, and mineral-rich soil of the Willamette Valley's location from Portland at its northern edge to Eugene in the south. Pinot Noir and Pinot Gris grapes have proven to be the stars in this land.

The conditions that make the Pacific Northwest so perfect for growing great wine grapes also support a wide array of culinary treasures. Dungeness crab and salmon from the icy Pacific waters, wild mushrooms from Northwest mountains and forests, lamb from Ellensburg, hazelnuts from the Willamette Valley, and peppers, asparagus, peaches, apples, cherries, and sweet onions from the eastern valleys of Washington—are all appreciated throughout the country and around the world.

IN THE REALM OF *New World regions, Chateau Ste. Michelle is truly a timeless classic— the founding winery of Washington State.*

Chateau Ste Michelle

IN MY TRAVELS, there is one thing I always tell people about Chateau Ste. Michelle: you must visit this winery. Chateau Ste. Michelle is the story of Washington wine—past, present, and future. Nowhere will you get such an immersion in winemaking, a history of a region and its vineyards, an opportunity to taste so many highly awarded wines—all in a setting that is simply spectacular. Chateau Ste. Michelle put Washington on the world wine map when it won a blind tasting of Rieslings in 1974. Since that time, the winery has consistently earned international recognition, and in 2009 was named a "Winery of the Year" by *Wine & Spirits* magazine for the fifteenth time. Only two other wineries in the world have earned as many.

The inspiration for the winery itself is a classic French chateau, but the beautiful grounds are unmistakably Northwest. The setting alone makes this winery a must-see. Set on an historic 87-acre wooded estate, Chateau Ste. Michelle is within easy reach of the Seattle area. Each year, more than 250,000 people enjoy winery tours and tastings, the historic grounds and garden tours, summer concerts, charity auctions, chef dinners, and a variety of other events. While you can easily spend the entire day at Chateau Ste. Michelle, if you find yourself with extra time there are many other tasting rooms, a brewery, and several wine-showcase restaurants in the neighborhood.

No matter what the season, a trip to Seattle would be incomplete without a visit to the winery that has played such an important role in the Pacific Northwest wine region. If you can plan ahead, check the Web site to see if you can take advantage of one of the many summer concerts, an Evening of Wine and Cheese, or an intimate seasonal multi-course Chef Dinner designed to showcase fresh Northwest ingredients, produce grown on the estate in the Chef's garden, and a wide range of Chateau Ste. Michelle wines.

JOHN SARICH

CHATEAU STE. MICHELLE— WASHINGTON STATE'S FOUNDING WINERY

Built on the 1912 estate owned by Seattle lumber baron Frederick Stimson, Chateau Ste. Michelle's roots date back to 1934 and the repeal of Prohibition. In that year both the Pommerelle Wine Company and the National Wine Company were formed. They merged in 1954 to form American Wine Growers. In 1967, American Wine Growers began a new line of premium vinifera wines called "Ste. Michelle Vintners" under the direction of legendary California winemaker André Tchelistcheff.

Ste. Michelle Vintners planted its first vines at Cold Creek Vineyard in Eastern Washington in 1972. Cold Creek remains one of the oldest and most renowned vineyards in the state.

The legendary André Tchelistcheff, one of the founding winemakers of Napa Valley, was a great believer in the potential of Washington State for world-class wines. He was very influential in bringing French vinifera grapes to Washington State and consulted with Chateau Ste. Michelle Winery for many years.

In 1976, Ste. Michelle Vintners built a French-style chateau in Woodinville, and changed its name to Chateau Ste. Michelle. As the winery grew, so did recognition for the increasingly top-quality wines being produced in Washington State. In 1984, Chateau Ste. Michelle led the way in obtaining federal recognition of the Columbia Valley in Eastern Washington as a unique wine-growing region or American Viticulture Area (AVA). Today, Chateau Ste. Michelle receives some of the highest accolades in the industry, fifteen wines named to *Wine Spectator*'s prestigious "Top 100 Wines of the Year" annual ranking, since 1994.

Chateau Ste. Michelle is perhaps best known as the leading American Riesling producer and has championed Riesling for more than forty years. The winery was catapulted into the international spotlight when its 1972 Johannisberg Riesling won the now famous Riesling blind tasting sponsored by the *Los Angeles Times* in 1974. Since 1999, the winery has partnered with renowned German wine pioneer, Ernst Loosen, to make the highly acclaimed Eroica Riesling.

LOCATION, LOCATION, LOCATION

Chateau Ste. Michelle is one of the few premium wineries in the world with two state-of-the-art wineries, one devoted to whites and another to reds.

THE 1912 MANOR HOUSE on Chateau Ste. Michelle's Woodinville estate was built as a summer home by lumber baron Frederick Stimson and is a registered historic landmark. Today several pieces of the winery's Artist Series glass art collection, including works by Dale Chihuly and Lino Tagliapietra, are on display there.

CLOCKWISE FROM TOP: *Merlot grapes from Chateau Ste. Michelle's Canoe Ridge Estate Vineyard consistently produce highly awarded wines; many small-lot bottlings are available exclusively at the winery's tasting room; delicate seafood dishes make savory companions to Chateau Ste. Michelle's signature Riesling wines.*

While all of Chateau Ste. Michelle's vineyards are located on the east side of the Cascade Mountains where the climate is dry and sunny, the award winning white wines are made in Woodinville, fifteen miles northeast of Seattle.

Chateau Ste. Michelle's red wines are made at its Canoe Ridge Estate Winery on the east side of the state, about two hundred miles from Seattle. Situated on a steep slope overlooking the Columbia River, the winery is in close proximity to Chateau Ste. Michelle's best vineyards including Cold Creek, Horse Heaven, and Canoe Ridge Estate.

"Washington is a unique place to grow and make wine," says winemaker Bob Bertheau. "The conditions in Eastern Washington are prefect for growing world-class grapes—low rainfall, lots of sunshine, weak soils, and warm temperatures. My winemaking goal is to preserve the fresh, fruit

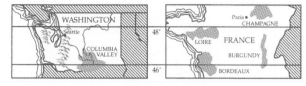

CHATEAU STE. MICHELLE was a pioneer in drawing the world's attention to the fact that Washington State's latitude and diverse growing conditions are very similar to parts of France and Germany.

character of the aromatic white varieties, while making them refined and elegant. For the red wines, our job is to harness our wonderfully structured fruit into harmonious and silky wines."

VISITING CHATEAU STE. MICHELLE

Chateau Ste. Michelle's Woodinville winery is one of the top visitor and historic attractions in the Seattle area. Located just fifteen miles northeast of Seattle, the winery is open daily for complimentary tours and tastings that appeal to novices and experts alike. For a small fee, guests can taste reserve and library wines as well. The winery Web site, www.ste-michelle.com, has a wealth of information on tour and tasting options, events, and other information, including a recipe database and a unique food and wine pairing resource.

CHATEAU STE. MICHELLE combines Old World wine-making tradition with New World innovation and is best known for its award-winning Riesling, Chardonnay, Merlot, and Cabernet Sauvignon. Columbia Valley wines are styled to bring out the varietal character of the region; Single Vineyard wines epitomize the terroir of the winery's best vineyards; Ethos wines are the winery's pinnacle tier; Eroica is a Washington Riesling made in collaboration with famed Mosel winemaker Ernst Loosen.

Chateau Ste. Michelle

Menu

Appetizer
Asian Dungeness Crab Cocktail
PAGE 82

Wine
Chateau Ste. Michelle
& Dr. Loosen Eroica Riesling

Entrée
Seared Alaska King Salmon
with Chanterelle Mushrooms
PAGE 142

Wines
Chateau Ste. Michelle
Indian Wells Chardonnay or
Canoe Ridge Estate Merlot

Dessert
Warm Berries over Ice Cream
PAGE 228

Wine
Chateau Ste. Michelle
Ethos Reserve Late Harvest
White Riesling

Chef's Notes

Like chefs everywhere, we try to use local seasonal ingredients to create our recipes. For me, it's not just the food from the area, but the regional wine and how they best match. There are so many great food products and wines to choose from in the Northwest that I thought for this menu we would focus on extravagant flavors and Northwest delicacies.

Rare is a day without several culinary events at the Chateau—in the intimate Chateau Library, historic Manor House, or the Grand Room—prepared by a dedicated and talented team of chefs who are passionate about their craft.

The Chateau culinary team prepared this special showcase menu for a taste of what guests might enjoy during a very special event at the winery.

FAVORITE INGREDIENTS

ASIAN DUNGENESS CRAB Cocktail is a favorite appetizer at the Chateau to complement the bright fruit and mineral notes of Riesling.

CHANTERELLE MUSHROOMS

Chanterelles are found in coniferous forests (of which there are many in Washington). The fungi depend on the roots of the tree to obtain nourishment and the tree benefits in the same way. They are considered one of the world's best mushrooms. Chanterelles appear in late summer to late fall, making them popular in fall harvest menus.

DUNGENESS CRAB

This popular delicacy gets its common name from the town of Dungeness, Washington, where the first commercial harvesting of the crab was done. Dungeness crab is the most significant commercial crab in the western states. This delicate seafood pairs beautifully with Chateau Ste. Michelle's signature Riesling.

RED RASPBERRIES

Grown in the northwestern part of Washington State on some of the country's most beautiful farmland, this wonderful fruit is packed with ellagic acid and rich in vitamin C—making raspberries one of the top-ranked antioxidant fruits. They are also high in fiber and nutrients. Washington State grows about 90 percent of the nation's total red raspberries—the majority in Whatcom County.

KING SALMON

Weighing in at an average of 30 pounds, the Chinook or "king salmon" is Washington's ultimate trophy fish. A king will spend anywhere from one to eight years at sea before returning home to spawn. They feed extensively before spawning runs, making them one of the richest and most delicious fish to eat. The Chinook salmon is Alaska's state fish.

Extravaganza Menu

**PREPARED BY EXECUTIVE CHEF JANET
HEDSTROM AND HER CULINARY TEAM**

FIRST COURSE
*Seared Wild King Salmon and Vegetables
in Asian Broth* – PAGE 156
Recipe by Executive Chef Janet Hedstrom

WINE
*Chateau Ste. Michelle
Cold Creek Vineyard Riesling*

SECOND COURSE
*"Shrooms on a Shingle" in
Chardonnay Cream Sauce* – PAGE 183
Recipe by Chef Kurt Olson

WINE
*Chateau Ste. Michelle
Ethos Reserve Chardonnay*

THIRD COURSE
*Grilled Quail with Poblano
Cornbread Pudding and Mole* – PAGE 165
Recipe by Chef Scott Harberts

WINE
Chateau Ste. Michelle Ethos Reserve Syrah

ENTRÉE
*Rib Eye Steak and Figs Grilled over
Grapevines with Cabernet Pan Sauce
& Arugula-Walnut Salad* – PAGE 206
Recipe by Chef Kim Marshall

WINES
*Chateau Ste. Michelle Artist Series
Meritage Red Wine
or Chateau Ste. Michelle Ethos
Reserve Cabernet Sauvignon*

DESSERT
*Orange-Infused Olive Oil Cake with Fresh Fruit
and Raspberry Coulis* – PAGE 240
Recipe by Chef Regina Paul-Jones

WINE
Chateau Ste. Michelle Late Harvest Chenin Blanc

QUAIL IS NOW *commonly available from many
specialty meat dealers. This magnificent bird is juicy,
moist, and perfect for grilling.*

CHATEAU STE. MICHELLE *Executive Chef
Janet Hedstrom (far right, middle row) and her
team prepare intimate, multi-course dinners
designed to showcase fresh Northwest ingredients
with special Chateau Ste. Michelle wines.*

LOCATED IN WASHINGTON
*State's Horse Heaven Hills,
Columbia Crest has grown
from a small winery in a
relatively unknown wine
region to one of the most
significant wineries in
America's history.*

COLUMBIA · CREST

I WAS RUNNING ADRIATICA, my restaurant in Seattle, when the Columbia Crest Winery opened in June of 1983. As a restaurateur, I was lucky enough to be invited to the grand opening celebration.

This winery was like nothing I had ever experienced (and I had been to many wineries by then). The view out over the vineyards to the Columbia River was beautiful. Entering the courtyard, I was charmed by the cobble-stone patio, the colorful flower boxes, and café tables. The casual elegance of the French-style winery was warm and inviting—still the essence of the Columbia Crest Winery today. But what lie ahead on our tour was the most amazing state-of-the-art wine-making facility I had ever seen. Ninety percent of the winery was built underground to maintain year-round temperature and humidity control.

I was awestruck by the size and scope of this winery and what it said about the future of Columbia Crest and Washington State wines. You might have thought that such a big winery couldn't make quality wine, but that was not the case. Over the years, the accolades given to Columbia Crest have been impressive. That confidence has proven to be well founded many times over. I think that Cabernet Sauvignon has been overlooked as a great wine from Washington. But in 2009, the 2005 Columbia Crest Reserve Cabernet Sauvignon was picked by *Wine Spectator* as the number one wine in their "Top 100 Wines of the Year" list. Of course, you won't be able to find the '05 Reserve Cabernet now, with that kind of recognition, but try Columbia Crest Walter Clore Private Reserve Red Wine, a Cabernet-based red blend. Also, for one of the best values in Washington Cabernet, you cannot go wrong with Columbia Crest Grand Estate Cabernet Sauvignon. Today there are more than six hundred Washington wineries. Many of their wines, including those of Columbia Crest, are sold all over the globe. Columbia Crest is one of the top selling and most highly awarded wineries in America.

JOHN SARICH

COLUMBIA CREST— WORLD RENOWNED; WASHINGTON GROWN

Located along the Columbia River in Eastern Washington's Horse Heaven Hills AVA, Columbia Crest is the Northwest's largest winery and one of the world's most highly acclaimed. The release of its 1984 vintage Merlot more than twenty years ago paved the way for Merlot to become the favorite "red" for wine consumers in America. Since that initial release, Columbia Crest's reputation has been built on delivering superior quality and value in all price ranges year after year.

Columbia Crest's story began in 1978 with the planting of 500 acres in Paterson, Washington. Here, in the southeastern part of the state where the Columbia River separates the Washington-Oregon border, the long warm summer days, cool nights, and very low rainfall provide the recipe for balanced wines.

With a firm belief that Washington wines would gain international recognition and demand, additional vineyards acres were planted each year until the estate reached its current 2,500 acres. In 1983, Columbia Crest opened its winery and visitor center overlooking the estate vineyards and the Columbia River. It remains one of the most beautiful estates in the world.

The next year, in 1984, official appellation (AVA) status was granted to Washington's Columbia Valley—the inspiration for the winery's name.

By 1990, Columbia Crest had been named one of the 24 "Best Value Wineries" in the world by Robert Parker's *The Wine Advocate* and one of the "Top Five U.S. Wineries" by *Impact* magazine. That same year, the *California Wine Experience* named Columbia Crest Merlot one of the "Top 10" wines in the world under eight dollars.

The winery was thrust onto the world stage in 1994 when the Columbia Crest 1990 Cabernet Sauvignon earned a gold medal at Challenge du Vin in Bordeaux, France—the only U.S. wine awarded a gold medal. And again, in 1997, the feat was repeated with the winery's 1994 Merlot. The

COLUMBIA CREST's *Two Vines, Grand Estates, Horse Heaven Hills (H3), and Reserve wines receive acclaim from critics and consumers alike for their food-friendly, approachable styles that capture the true expression of each grape variety.*

"CREATING WINES THAT *surpass people's expectations is what motivates me. Columbia Crest excels on two fronts: delivering world-class, handcrafted, small-lot wines as well as wines that are widely available. People don't expect Columbia Crest to offer both ends of the spectrum. The thrill for me is constantly delivering wines that beat expectations."*

RAY EINBERGER, COLUMBIA CREST WINEMAKER

world was increasingly taking note of the quality of red wines from Washington.

In 2008, Columbia Crest celebrated its twenty-fifth anniversary. A fitting tribute to that milestone, *Wine Spectator* rated the Columbia Crest 2005 Reserve Cabernet Sauvignon "95 points," the highest score the winery had ever received.

VISITING COLUMBIA CREST

This picture-perfect winery, with its beautiful grounds overlooking estate vineyards and the nearby Columbia River, is an ideal setting for a picnic and a leisurely afternoon. Columbia Crest offers visitors a self-guided tour of the winery and complimentary tastings seven days a week. Adjacent to the tasting room is a magnificent patio. There is no better time to visit than fall when harvest is in full swing: watching the grapes roll in to be crushed, smelling their ripe sweetness, and enjoying the bustling activity is a wonderful experience. Check the winery's Web site, www.columbia-crest.com, for more information, a list of events, and driving directions from Seattle, Portland, and Spokane.

Chef's Notes

Columbia Crest excels with such a wide range of wines that trying multiple wines with a single course conveys the versatility of styles. The appetizer may feature the signature Grand Estates Chardonnay or Sauvignon Blanc, but can also work well with the Two Vines Shiraz or Rose. A full-flavored meat entrée such as Flat Iron Steak can be enjoyed with several different red wines such as Columbia Crest Reserve Cabernet Sauvignon, Grand Estates Merlot or Cabernet, and Walter Clore Private Reserve Red Wine.

IN 2009, *Columbia Crest's 2005 Reserve Cabernet Sauvignon was awarded the number 1 spot on* Wine Spectator's *prestigious "Top 100 Wines of the Year."*

FAVORITE INGREDIENTS

APPLES

By 1826, early settlers in Eastern Washington State had discovered that the area's dry climate, rich lava-ash soil, and plentiful sunshine created perfect conditions for growing apples. Today, ten to twelve billion apples are hand-picked in Washington State each year. Washington State grows more than 60 percent of the apples commercially sold in the U.S.

PEACHES

From July to September, Washington's more than four hundred peach growers will visit their trees between five and seven times to harvest twenty thousand tons of fruit as it reaches its peak of ripeness. Like the wine-grape growers, peach growers will measure the peaches' degree of sugar to acid and pick during the time of optimal ripeness and juiciness.

MORELS

Possibly the most hunted, most cherished wild mushroom in North America. Morels grow exceptionally well in pine forests on the east side of Washington's Cascade Range, but for only a few weeks each spring. The earthy flavored delicacy, which has an unusual cone shape and pitted texture similar to a pine cone, can range in size from one to six inches.

Menu

APPETIZER
Grilled Peaches with Prosciutto
PAGE 84

WINE
*Columbia Crest Two Vines
Sauvignon Blanc*

ENTRÉE
Flat Iron Steak
PAGE 196
with Potatoes, Peppers, and Onions
PAGE 215

WINES
*Columbia Crest
Walter Clore Private Reserve Red Wine
or Columbia Crest Grand Estates
Cabernet Sauvignon*

DESSERT
*Apple Strudel
with Dried Cherries and Raisins*
PAGE 226

NATURALLY NORTHWEST
Wines—connected to the
earth, crafted by a veteran
Washington winemaker,
using pristine fruit from
healthy vineyards for over
two decades.

SNOQUALMIE

Driving through the heart of Washington wine country, you will find the Snoqualmie Winery located in the small town of Prosser. It's just about a three-hour drive east of Seattle, but it feels like a different world. Here the sun shines almost daily, the pace is slow, and people greet strangers like old friends. I always find myself slowing down just a bit when I'm here. And I start thinking produce. Produce stands dot the area with an abundance of fruits and vegetables. Prosser is home to the largest variety of crops in Washington State. Not surprisingly, wine grapes grow exceptionally well here.

Organic farming is expanding quickly, although Snoqualmie winemaker Joy Andersen has forged a strong relationship between Snoqualmie wines and organic and sustainable vineyard practices for years. The Snoqualmie "Naked" wines, made with certified organically grown grapes in a certified organic facility, are in strong demand.

Restaurateurs have embraced local, fresh, sustainable, and organic practices for a long time. Now they are happily welcoming wines like those from Snoqualmie that meet these same standards while delivering top quality.

I respect Joy and her team for their stance on sustainability and for taking an active interest in the local environment. Snoqualmie is committed to taking good care of their vineyards. This approach ensures the continued natural beauty of the land and the natural quality of their wines. Joy's philosophy to "keep it simple" has led to the creation of elegant, award-winning wines. Like a master chef, Joy pays special attention to the ingredients that go into her creations. Since Snoqualmie brings to my mind thoughts of a fresh day in the outdoors, to this end I've created a natural, alfresco meal for your enjoyment.

John Sarich

SNOQUALMIE WINERY—
NATURALLY NORTHWEST

Snoqualmie Winery, named after the mountain pass that serves as the gateway to Washington wine country, has been making food-friendly wines that reflect the balance and natural beauty of the Pacific Northwest for more than two decades.

Rich in the heritage of the land, yet committed to growing techniques that are sustainable and organic, Snoqualmie wines reflect the people who tend the vineyards—straightforward and honest. Snoqualmie uses farming practices in its vineyards that ensure the health of the soil and vines, keeping them fertile for many years to come. Amid rolling hills, grapes ripen under intensely blue skies, cared for by families who have lived on the land and worked it for generations. The scenery has not changed much in the last hundred years, and with care, it will remain unchanged.

"I THINK TRYING to let the fruit come through in the wine without extra magic or processing is the best way to showcase each varietal. Great wines are about understanding when to relinquish control to Mother Nature; we can do little to improve her bounty."

JOY ANDERSEN, SNOQUALMIE WINEMAKER

SNOQUALMIE MAKES *its home in the small farming town of Prosser, Washington and the surrounding Yakima Valley. This is one of the nation's most bountiful farm regions, producing cherries, peaches, apples, pears, plums, peppers, and great wine.*

"Naked" Wine

The "Naked" wines are made with certified organically grown grapes in a certified organic facility, and all of Snoqualmie's wines are made with minimal intervention using sustainable and organic techniques. The Columbia Valley wines offer fruit intensity and classic varietal flavors that are ready to be enjoyed now. Snoqualmie's Reserve wines showcase the best wine-making techniques and vineyard selections.

Snoqualmie was one of first wineries in Washington to craft wines from USDA-certified organically grown grapes, and as of 2009 has the largest certified organic vineyard in the state. The winery has deep roots in the vineyards and in the community. Each September, Snoqualmie hosts an annual Greener Living and Harvest Celebration at the winery in Prosser. The event showcases local green businesses and products, locally produced foods paired with Snoqualmie's Naked wines, and live jazz.

Visiting Snoqualmie Winery

Prosser is about a three-hour drive from Seattle. The scenery along the way is dramatic, changing from towering evergreens and mountain peaks to rolling hills, vineyards, and orchards. Although the winery hosts events throughout the year, Snoqualmie's unpretentious and quintessentially Northwest tasting room and patio make a pleasant stop any time while visiting Washington wine country. The winery is open for tastings seven days a week. For more information about visiting Snoqualmie and a list of winery events, see the winery's Web site at www.snoqualmie.com.

Chef's Notes

The clean, straight-forward flavors of Snoqualmie wines do not require heavy, complex foods, hence this informal menu. Sometimes the simplest food can bring out the best in the wines. Snoqualmie Naked Riesling can go with almost any food—try it with the Heirloom Tomato Salad. For the chicken, Naked Merlot or Chardonnay makes a great accompaniment.

Favorite Ingredients

TREE FRUIT

The dry climate, long, sun-filled days, and cool nights in Eastern Washington, ideal for growing wine grapes, also make ideal growing conditions for fruit trees, including cherry, apple, and pear trees. In fact, many of the state's grape growers are also significant fruit growers.

SNOQUALMIE'S "NAKED" wines are pure expressions of the vineyards in which they were grown—fresh and clean, with all the bright flavors of Mother Nature's palette.

SNOQUALMIE

Menu

APPETIZER
Heirloom Tomato Salad
PAGE 116

WINE
*Snoqualmie Naked Riesling,
Columbia Valley*

ENTRÉE
Roasted Rosemary Chicken
PAGE 172
with Warm Potato Salad
PAGE 127

WINE
*Snoqualmie
Naked Chardonnay,
Columbia Valley*

DESSERT
Apple and Pear Compote
PAGE 232

TWO UNIQUE WINE *cultures, one extraordinary Washington wine.*

COL SOLARE

The inaugural release of Col Solare in 1999 was highly anticipated. There had never been a partnership in Washington like it—a collaboration between Chateau Ste. Michelle and Italy's famed winemaker, Marchese Piero Antinori. For the opening celebration I was in charge of the special dinner to commemorate the event.

Over the years, I have cooked for many famous people. Even with my Mediterranean background, cooking for an Italian of the Marchese's stature was a bit daunting to me since this is a man who is revered in wine and food circles. The event was a celebration, a joining of families. In the end, I decided on a menu I would be comfortable serving and celebrating with family in my home.

After the pasta course, Bolognese Pappardelle, the winery's president came into the kitchen to say the Marchese wanted to speak with the chef. I had no idea what to expect. After a gracious hello and thank you, he gave a broad smile and said, "You can cook pasta for me any day!"

Col Solare is a Cabernet Sauvignon-based wine with concentrated flavors, supple tannins, and a seductive, lingering finish. It is a wine that welcomes bold foods like herb-seasoned lamb, Tuscan steak, or smoked duck breast with a good pasta. To this day, I enjoy Bolognese Pappardelle with a bottle of Col Solare whenever I can. It always makes me smile.

John Sarich

COL SOLARE—A WASHINGTON WINE WITH A TUSCAN SOUL

Marchese Piero Antinori, known for his life-long curiosity about how grapes are grown around the world, journeyed from his home in Florence, Italy to Washington's Columbia Valley in 1992 at the urging of André Tchelistcheff, also a wine industry legend.

TOASTING THE NEW *Col Solare Winery and Estate Vineyard on Grand Opening day, April 12, 2007, are Marchese Piero Antinori (on right) and Ted Baseler, President and CEO of Ste. Michelle Wine Estates. They share a goal to unite two unique viticultural and wine-making cultures to create a luxury Cabernet Sauvignon-based wine.*

During the trip, Antinori discovered an emerging wine region, supported by the zealous leadership of Chateau Ste. Michelle, the Northwest's oldest and most-acclaimed winery, highly regarded for its innovative work within its vineyards and winery.

Antinori, whose family has been making wine for twenty-six generations, helped create the Italian Super Tuscan category with his Tignanello and Solaia wines. In the vineyards of Washington's Columbia Valley, he found Old World character, structure, and fruit expression. He turned to Chateau Ste. Michelle to form a partnership based on the mutual pursuit of shared grape-growing and wine-making philosophies.

This partnership introduced Col Solare, Italian for "shining hill," with the 1995 vintage. With Cabernet Sauvignon set as the dominant variety, the partners worked closely to forge their two distinct grape-growing and wine-making cultures into Col Solare's powerful yet elegant style.

In 2000, Piero Antinori and Ste. Michelle's Ted Baseler decided to build a winery properly scaled and singularly focused on Col Solare to best achieve the wine's extraordinary potential.

They considered several premier sites before choosing Red Mountain, one of the Columbia Valley's smallest, but most celebrated, sub-appellations, known for its Cabernet Sauvignon.

The Col Solare winery celebrated its grand opening in April of 2007. The refined state-of-the-art winery, built from sustainable materials, is a dramatic confluence of winemaking and architecture. It sits majestically towards the top of the 1,500 foot Red Mountain and enjoys panoramic views of Mt. Adams, Mt. Rainier, the Horse Heaven Hills, and the valley below. The winery's distinctive bell tower is reminiscent of Tuscany, while the 300-foot-long and 25-foot-high stone wall emulates the basalt cliffs of the Columbia Valley. Combined with clean and contemporary lines in the rest of the building, the winery beauti-

WINEMAKER MARCUS NOTARO collaborates with Antinori to produce Col Solare. "Our goal is to achieve a balanced wine with a concentration of flavors and complexity. Our philosophy is to blend the wines early, based on tasting trials that begin in the vineyard."

fully expresses both Old and New World inspiration. Completing the unique estate are 30 acres of vineyards, which radiate from the winery, down the slope of the hill like rays of the sun—an expression of the "shining hill" in Col Solare's name.

VISITING COL SOLARE

A visit to the Col Solare winery can be arranged by private appointment. An hour-long private tour and tasting provides the history of this unique partnership during a tour of the estate vineyard, winery, and cellars. There will be time to enjoy the expansive view from the Red Mountain tasting room while sampling two vintages of Col Solare for a side-by-side taste comparison. A longer ninety-minute private tour with formal pairings is also available. This experience combines the comprehensive estate tour and a sampling of current and past vintages of Col Solare with an array of gourmet cheeses and cured meats selected to pair with the wine. More information can be found at www.colsolare.com. Appointments can be made by calling (509) 588-6806 or sending an e-mail to: info@colsolare.com

Chef's Notes

With the "Italian accent" of Col Solare, putting together an Italian accented menu seemed natural. The people of Tuscany are sometimes known as the "bean people" for the use of beans in their foods. I prepared this menu for the winery's grand opening celebration. The dishes complement the wine beautifully.

COL SOLARE is a Cabernet Sauvignon based wine with concentrated flavors, supple tannins, and a seductive, lingering finish. It is a wine that welcomes bold foods like like herb-seasoned lamb or Tuscan steak.

FAVORITE INGREDIENTS

BEANS AND PULSES

The generic term pulses includes beans, peas, and legumes. There are twenty species of beans commonly grown for food, including white, green, black, brown, red, adzuki, lima, fava, and soy. Though part of the Fabaceae family, legumes are different and include certain peas, garbanzos, and lentils. Lentils are a huge class of their own and the Northwest grows the largest crop of lentils in the U.S., over 40 percent of the country's production.

PEPPERS

Though there are less than 500 acres of warm-weather loving peppers grown in Washington State, Yakima County is the state's leading producer. Peppers come in many varieties, colors, and sizes, but there are two main types of peppers: hot and sweet. Botanically, bell peppers are fruits, but for culinary purposes they are considered as vegetables.

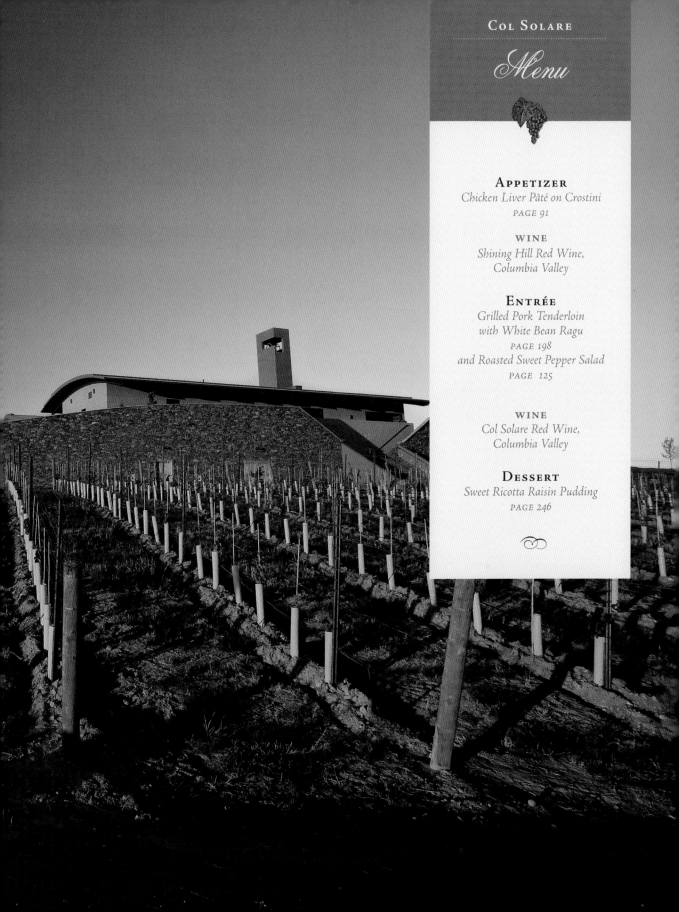

COL SOLARE

Menu

APPETIZER
Chicken Liver Pâté on Crostini
PAGE 91

WINE
*Shining Hill Red Wine,
Columbia Valley*

ENTRÉE
*Grilled Pork Tenderloin
with White Bean Ragu*
PAGE 198
and Roasted Sweet Pepper Salad
PAGE 125

WINE
*Col Solare Red Wine,
Columbia Valley*

DESSERT
Sweet Ricotta Raisin Pudding
PAGE 246

NORTHSTAR IS
DEDICATED *to the
production of
ultra-premium Merlot,
showcasing Washington's
star grape variety.*

NORTHSTAR

W ALLA WALLA is arguably one of the most quaint and attractive wine areas in the Pacific Northwest. A four-and-a-half-hour drive southeast from Seattle, Walla Walla is known for producing elegant, bold red wines among more than one hundred boutique wineries. The city itself has an award-winning historic downtown with upscale restaurants, boutiques, galleries, cafés, and tasting rooms. As the town has grown, so too have the number of bed and breakfasts, small inns, and hotels. Reminiscent of an earlier Napa Valley, Walla Walla offers a perfect food and wine getaway.

Northstar is a winery you will not want to miss when visiting Walla Walla. Most wineries make wines from each of several grape varieties, so when a winery chooses to focus on just one variety you know it is something special. Northstar has devoted itself to Merlot—really incredible Merlot. Visiting a winery with a single focus is quite a different experience and I highly recommend it. The tasting experience focuses on differences in vintages or vineyards and provides a great way to learn more about wine.

Merlot-based wines from Bordeaux's Pomerol region have long been the gold standard of red wine. They are generally the most expensive, sought-after wines in the world. Furthermore, Merlot continues to be the best selling red wine in America, for good reason. Merlot can be delicious and complex and juicy and robust. That is, given the right place to grow the grapes and the right wine-making know-how. At Northstar, you'll find Merlot is all these things. My favorite place to sip on a glass of Northstar Merlot is on the Northstar Winery patio overlooking one of the most beautiful scenes in the Northwest—the Blue Mountains. Pure inspiration.

JOHN SARICH

NORTHSTAR WINERY— WORLD CLASS MERLOT

Northstar's promise is that only the best of the best Columbia Valley and Walla Walla Valley grapes are chosen for Northstar Merlot. These viticultural areas have put Washington State on the world map of best Merlot-producing regions. The result is a wine comparable to Prestige Cru Classé level wines from the Pomerol and St. Emilion regions—wines that achieve the pinpoint balance between power and finesse from grapes grown at the same latitude.

Since the inaugural 1994 vintage, Northstar has been making Merlots that are among the most highly acclaimed in the world by blending New World fruit with an Old World wine-making style. Winemaker David "Merf" Merfeld, who arrived at Northstar in 2001, utilizes both science—in the form of cutting-edge equipment and research—and the blender's art to create Northstar's award-winning Merlots.

Vineyard diversity is one of the keys to Northstar's success. For any given vintage, nearly two dozen unique vineyard blocks from around the Columbia Valley are sourced, with a dozen or so making it through the rigorous selection process into the final blend. The majority of these vineyards are over fifteen years old (vine maturity is important for Merlot and Cabernet grapes) and are farmed to the wine-making team's specifications.

Northstar produces three wines: the flagship Columbia Valley Merlot; the limited production Walla Walla Merlot, which showcases fruit only from the Walla Walla sub-appellation and from the Northstar Estate Vineyard; and Stella Maris, a Columbia Valley red wine blended from wines made for Northstar's Merlot blends, but ultimately not selected for the final blend.

VISITING NORTHSTAR

Surrounded by its estate vineyard and nestled in the foothills of the scenic Blue Mountains, Northstar is just a short drive from Walla Walla's historic downtown area. Visitors are welcome seven days a week for tours of the state-of-the-art winery and tastings of award-winning Merlots. Several winery-only releases are available to taste as well. Whether seated around the dramatic centerpiece fireplace or outside on the patio, a glass of Northstar wine is a perfect pairing with the beautiful panorama of the mountains. Northstar participates in Walla Walla's Spring and Holiday Barrel Tasting weekends and hosts several events throughout the year. Events include special dinners in the Petit Chai, music, vertical tastings of past vintages, and private events for its wine club members. More information can be found at www.northstarmerlot.com.

Northstar wines were voted favorites over prestige French competitors at a Miami taste-off. Merlots from Northstar winery bested Merlot-based wines from premier Bordeaux producers Châteaux Cheval Blanc, Pavie, Angelus, Trotanoy, and La Conseillante in a blind comparative tasting at the South Beach Wine and Food Festival in Miami in 2009.

NORTHSTAR HAS FOUND that diverse vineyard locations make for more interesting wines. More than fifteen distinct vineyard blocks are carefully watched through the growing season—row by row, vine by vine. Each block is carefully selected for a unique dimension it will bring to the finished wine—either distinct aromas and flavors or structure and tannins.

WALLA WALLA *was named after a Native American expression meaning "many waters." Walla Walla sits in the foothills of the Blue Mountains in the souteastern corner of Washington State. Abundant waters flowing down from the Blue Mountains help provide irrigation for the many vineyards, fruit orchards, and wheat fields in the area.*

Chef's Notes

When pairing a complex wine like Northstar, the uncomplicated flavor of the dish can best show off the wine. In my home state of Washington, we love to pair Merlot with our most popular local foods. This menu features local produce and lamb. Add a sauce made from Washington cherries to the lamb and you are in heaven.

FAVORITE INGREDIENTS

WALLA WALLA SWEET ONIONS

The Walla Walla Sweet Onion came to the area as a seed from Corsica, brought by a French soldier over a century ago and cultivated by Italian immigrants who formed the core of Walla Walla's gardening industry. It is prized for its exceptional sweetness, jumbo size, and round shape. In 2007, it became the official state vegetable.

CHERRIES

More than half of all the cherries grown in the U.S. come from the bountiful cherry trees of Washington State. Annually over 170 million tons of cherries are harvested each year, including the vibrant Bing, the early-ripening Chelan, and the sweet Rainier cherry.

NORTHSTAR'S COLUMBIA VALLEY Merlot is a rich wine that is concentrated and yet elegant. The emphasis is always on the bright cherry fruit that gives Washington Merlot its immediate appeal. Northstar's limited production Walla Walla Merlot is a blend of Merlot and Cabernet Sauvignon exclusively from local Walla Walla vineyard sites.

NORTHSTAR

Menu

APPETIZER
Sweet Onion and Tomato Salad
PAGE 126

ENTRÉE
Herbed Leg of Lamb
with Sweet Cherry Sauce
PAGE 192
with Risi e Bisi
PAGE 220

WINE
Northstar
Merlot, Columbia Valley

DESSERT
Apple Custard Mousse
with Cherries
PAGE 236

A FAMILY HERITAGE
and a unique fingerprint
of its land, captured
in true estate wines.

WALLA WALLA

SPRING VALLEY VINEYARD

WASHINGTON

SPRING VALLEY VINEYARD has deep roots in its corner of the Walla Walla Valley. This is a very special place with really special people. The Corkrum-Derby family has farmed here for generations; from Uriah Corkrum to his son Frederick and Frederick's wife, Nina Lee, onto daughter Shari and her husband, Dean Derby. Each one of the Spring Valley Vineyard wines is named for one of the ancestors.

I love to drive the extra ten to twelve miles outside of town to visit the ranch and the people here. Winemaker Serge Laville will stop and chat if he can, but since it is a small working winery he is usually bustling about. That is why the winery opened a tasting room in downtown Walla Walla. There is no pretension here—just great family homesteading stories and outstanding wines. The winery is small and rustic, but it is authentic, charming, and full of history.

Near Spring Valley in the Walla Walla area, lamb is still being raised, and as in most wine-growing areas of the world, the food that grows there, goes with the wine produced from the grapes that grow there.

Like their namesakes, each of the wines has a completely unique, larger-than-life character. The site proved to be ideal for wine almost as soon as the first grapes were harvested. This little winery from the corner of Washington State turned heads by earning a spot on *Wine Spectator*'s "TOP 100 Wines of the Year" annual ranking with its first vintage of 2003 Uriah. It was just the first of many TOP 100 testimonials that have followed.

JOHN SARICH

SPRING VALLEY VINEYARD— A TRUE ESTATE WINERY

Rough-hewn, almost Spartan, Spring Valley Vineyard is a true estate winery, which means only fruit grown on its 44-acre vineyard goes into its wines. Flourishing in the optimal sunshine, wind, and drainage, the vines bask in the reflective nature of the surrounding wheat fields.

The land that the Corkrum-Derby family farms today is rich with history dating back to 1865, when Shari Corkrum Derby's grandfather, Uriah Corkrum, began farming in the area. After much success farming in Washington's Walla Walla Valley in the 1880s, Uriah lost everything in the economic depression of 1893, but persevered and acquired the property that became Spring Valley Ranch and Vineyard in the early 1900s. The family wheat farm continues today.

In 1993, the family planted grapevines adjacent to their wheat fields. In 1995, Walla Walla area winemakers began using Spring Valley Vineyard grapes for their select wines. Shari and Dean Derby took notice, and with their son, Devin Corkrum Derby, decided to open the winery and produce estate-bottled wines beginning with the 1999 vintage. Devin built the winery and served as winemaker until his untimely death in 2004, after which his friend and longtime assistant Serge Laville, a classically trained French winemaker, took over as Spring Valley Vineyard winemaker. Today, Laville continues to make wines in the traditional style he and Devin Derby both believed in: farming superior grapes and using as little winemaker intervention as possible.

The small winery was thrust into the national spotlight when its very first release, the 2003 Uriah, earned a score of 94 points and a place on the *Wine Spectator*'s prestigious "TOP 100 Wines of the Year" in 2006. Since that first release, the wines of Spring Valley Vineyard have consistently earned the coveted

SPRING VALLEY VINEYARD *is a limited production winery, producing only Estate grown and bottled red wine. The names given to the wines are a tribute to the family members who have struggled and succeeded in farming the same land where Spring Valley Vineyard now flourishes. Pictured from top to bottom: Shari Corkrum Derby riding with her father, Frederick, on the ranch; the plows were pulled by a mule team and driven by the "muleskinner"; Frederick and his wife, Nina Lee, on the ranch circa 1930.*

THREE TIMES EACH DAY, in order to extract maximum flavor during fermentation, winemaker Serge Laville punches down the cap of grape skins that float to the top.

LOCATED ON LATITUDE 46° North, the Walla Walla Valley straddles the line between the Burgundy and Bordeaux regions of France. The long hot summer days and short cool nights produce a perfect balance of sugars and acidity in the grapes. Additionally, this high latitude means that grapes are able to remain on the vine weeks after they must be harvested in most other regions. This allows the flavors to intensify and gain complexity.

90+ scores from wine publications, testimony to the exceptional land that the family founded and has successfully cultivated.

VISITING SPRING VALLEY VINEYARD

Spring Valley Vineyard wines are available in the quaint downtown Walla Walla tasting room, and no appointments are necessary Thursday through Monday. The unique charm of the tasting room lies in the generations of Corkrum-Derby family history lining the walls and in the stories often told by the staff. It is easy to make a full day of the downtown area after visiting the tasting room—shops, restaurants, cafés, galleries, and many other tasting rooms are within walking distance, so plan ahead. A visit to the Spring Valley Vineyard ranch, located twenty minutes northeast of downtown in rural Walla Walla, requires an appointment. An ideal time to visit the estate is for one of several special events hosted there during the year. More information is located on the winery's Web site at www.springvalleyvineyard.com.

Chef's Notes

Spring Valley Vineyard wines are full bodied and packed with intense fruit. I like to serve them with full-flavored meat dishes using simple preparations that allow the lusciousness of the fruit to shine through. Freshly baked bread made from cracked wheat is a favorite accompaniment to this menu.

URIAH IS A MERLOT blend named for Uriah Corkrum, farmer and rancher of Spring Valley. Frederick is a Cabernet Sauvignon blend named for Frederick Corkrum, son on Uriah. At age 12, Frederick began driving the mules that pulled the wheat combine; he was considered the head mule skinner. Muleskinner, a 100 percent Merlot wine, is also named in honor of Frederick.

FAVORITE INGREDIENTS

WHEAT

It would be hard to imagine life without this staple, which has been an integral part of our diet. During the 1880s Walla Walla underwent a wheat-growing boom on the heels of the gold rush. Especially successful was the practice of dryland wheat farming, begun around 1864, on the hills surrounding the city. Wheat became the backbone of Walla Walla's economy. Today wheat is Washington State's number one field crop and number one agricultural export.

PROSCIUTTO

As an excellent appetizer to serve with wine, include cured meats such as thin slices of Italian prosciutto—probably the world's most famous dry-cured ham. Also try Coppa, Serrano ham, Bresaola (salted beef), and sweet and spicy salamis—all superb accompaniments when wine tasting. Dry-curing involves salting the meat and keeping it at a cool temperature, about 55° F, for several months.

SPRING VALLEY VINEYARD

Menu

APPETIZER
Prosciutto-wrapped Stuffed Dates
PAGE 100

WINE
*Spring Valley Vineyard
Muleskinner Merlot,
Walla Walla Valley*

ENTRÉE
*Braised Lamb Shanks in
Syrah with Polenta*
PAGE 189
and Baby Broccoli Sauté
PAGE 212

WINE
*Spring Valley Vineyard
Uriah Red Wine, Walla Walla Valley
or Spring Valley Vineyard
Nina Lee Syrah, Walla Walla Valley*

DESSERT
*Chocolate Mousse
with Cabernet Syrup*
PAGE 230

THERE'S A PLACE IN
Oregon wine country
where EARTH and HEART
intersect. It's called ERATH,
the original winery of the
Dundee Hills of Oregon.

ERATH
WINERY

Erath Winery is one of the founding Oregon Pinot Noir wineries, and it was Dick Erath who planted the first grapevines in the Dundee Hills more than forty years ago. We owe a lot to this pioneer and the others that followed. The Northwest wine industry would not be what it is today without Oregon Pinot Noir. Washington's geography, climate, and soil are ideal for most classic wine grapes, but Pinot Noir requires much different conditions. Erath discovered how extremely well suited Oregon's cooler climate is for this tempermental grape.

I love creating menus around Pinot Noir. With its bright acidity and gentle tannins, it is such a perfect food wine. Classic Oregon Pinots are elegant, lighter in body, and fruit driven. It pairs well with foods like roasted poultry and seafood, but can stand up to many meat dishes as well. Erath produces some small-lot Single Vineyard Pinots that are bigger, richer wines for great Northwest food and wine pairing options.

A visit to Oregon Pinot country is an easy drive from Portland. Soon you are out of the city and into lush, green rolling hills, framed by mountains and dotted with vineyards. It is completely distinct from Washington or California wine countries. The wineries are mostly small, laid back, and genuinely friendly. A visit to Erath and its neighbors is well worth it when you are in the Northwest.

JOHN SARICH

ERATH WINERY—A PINOT PIONEER

Erath wines are an expression of the land that the winery has cultivated for more than forty years, longer than any other winery in the Dundee Hills of Oregon. The red, iron-rich Jory soils, combined with gentle breezes and warming sunshine of a marine climate, have bestowed upon Dundee a terroir of note. It has given rise to the hand-crafting phenomenon, and the art of Pinot.

As one of Oregon's wine pioneers, Dick Erath had always been as tenacious in his approach to Pinot as the Pinot grape is stubborn. The engineer-turned-viticulturist was first inspired to pursue winemaking in 1965 after an early garage experiment. After completing coursework at UC Davis in 1968, Erath relocated his family from California to the untamed red hills of Dundee. An unheated logger's cabin on 49 acres would serve as home—and ad hoc winery—for several years.

The following spring, he planted the Dundee Hill's first wine grapes. Pinot Noir flourished. By 1972, Erath had produced his first commercial wine of 216 cases—the first official wine production in the Dundee Hills. Enchanted with French varietals, he soon began testing non-California clones and was instrumental in importing French clones to Oregon in 1974.

In 1976, Erath broke ground on the first winery in the Dundee Hills. Early successes, including the 1982 Pinot Noir vintage which was named "Best American Pinot Noir" by *Wine & Spirits Magazine*, inspired leading winemakers to move to Oregon to forge their own path in this special place. In 2007, Erath's 2005 Estate Selection Pinot Noir was named to *Wine Spectator*'s prestigious "Top 100 Wines of the Year" annual ranking.

Current winemaker Gary Horner's philosophy is to craft high-quality wines that are fruit forward and reflect the vintage, soil, and grapes. Gary, who worked with Dick Erath, is committed to making the best Pinot that Oregon has to offer.

The 1960s ushered in an era of wine-making adventurists in Oregon. A yet undiscovered pearl along the 45° North latitude—that imaginary line that encircles the globe, stringing together such legendary northern wine regions as France's Côtes du Rhône and Italy's Piedmont—Oregon's Willamette Valley lured a few young mavericks. Among them was Dick Erath who planted his first Pinot Noir grapes in the Dundee Hills in the heart of the Willamette Valley.

PINOT NOIR GRAPES *thrive in the northern latitude of Oregon's Willamette Valley. Occasional marine breezes and long hours of sunshine allow grapes to ripen gradually, which is key to producing memorable wines. Erath sources grapes from vineyards throughout the Dundee Hills and across the appellations of Oregon —this land is the palette from which Erath creates the art of Pinot Noir.*

VISTING THE ESTATE

An easy thirty-mile drive southwest from Portland, Erath is located in Dundee, Oregon. Here you can savor classic Oregon Pinot while enjoying the rustic charm of the surroundings and the sweeping views of the picturesque Jory hills from the winery's patio. The tasting room is open daily and guests have the option of a complimentary tasting, or for a small fee guests can taste special winery-only releases or small-lot single vineyard wines. Tours and private tastings require an appointment by calling (800) 539-9463. More information about Erath and seasonal events at the winery are available on the Web site at www.erath.com.

THE WINERY OFFERS three distinct styles of Pinot Noir: the Oregon Pinot is soft and fruit forward for early drinking and enjoyment; the Estate Selection is a blend that highlights the finesse, balance, and complexity of the best vineyard sites in Oregon, and small-lot single vineyard Pinots are crafted to showcase the unique characteristics of single vineyard sites. The winery also produces Pinot Gris and Pinot Blanc, cool-climate white wines that are fresh, lively, and fruit driven.

Chef's Notes

Oregon, like much of the Pacific Coast, has local ingredients that Oregonians proudly claim as their own. Game, rabbit, and seafood are just a few. When the morels come out in the spring, chefs look to Oregon as a premium area. Blueberries are another treat that is used in the regional cooking of Oregon.

Combining Oregon Pinot Noir and braised rabbit is a perfect marriage of Oregon ingredients. Definitely try Pinot Noir with salmon and another Oregon product—hazelnuts. (Hazelnuts are also known as filberts. The name is connected with the day that the harvesting of the nuts traditionally began in Europe—St. Philbert's day, which falls on April 22.)

FAVORITE INGREDIENT

HAZELNUTS

Ninety-eight percent of all hazelnuts grown in the United States come from the rich soil of the Willamette Valley in Oregon. Also known as the filbert (which is the correct name for the tree and nut) this nut was likely first introduced into Oregon by early French settlers. According to a manuscript found in China, from the year 2838 B.C., the filbert took its place among the five sacred nourishments God bestowed on human beings. A slow roasting over low temperature intensifies the unique flavor of hazelnuts and develops their color.

ERATH WINERY

Menu

APPETIZER
Prosciutto Salad Rolls
PAGE 124

WINE
Erath
Oregon Pinot Gris

ENTRÉE
Braised Rabbit with Pinot Noir
and Dried Cherries
PAGE 190

WINE
Erath
Estate Selection Pinot Noir

DESSERT
Oregon Blueberry Tart
with Hazelnut Topping
PAGE 241

CALIFORNIA

CALIFORNIA, KNOWN FOR its world-class wines, is the fourth leading wine-producing region in the world behind France, Italy, and Spain. The words "Napa Valley" have become synonymous with great California wine. Although it is the most renowned AVA (American Viticulture Area) in the United States, the Napa Valley is also one of the smallest and most diverse wine-growing regions in the world.

Napa Valley enjoys a Mediterranean climate, which covers only two percent of the earth's surface. This climate, along with very diverse and complex soils, is ideal for growing wine grapes. Although the Napa Valley is an area running only thirty miles long and a few miles wide, the varied topography ranges from flat valley floor to steep mountain slopes and high plateaus. There are fifteen approved sub-appellations within the Napa Valley AVA, each recognized for its own unique characteristics.

Cabernet Sauvignon has been deemed "king" in Napa Valley. The fact is, the area is so diverse that many grape varieties thrive here. Beyond Cabernet Sauvignon, a range of wines are grown in the Napa Valley including Merlot, Pinot Noir, Chardonnay, Sauvignon Blanc, Zinfandel, Sangiovese, and Cabernet Franc. In the early years of winemaking in Napa Valley, grapes were often planted with many varieties mixed in a single vineyard. But experience has since shown vintners which grapes grow best in each location.

A temperate climate all year round makes California the number one food and agricultural producer in the United States. And wine is the state's number one finished agricultural product. California is well known for avocados, artichokes, eggplant, ripe olives, almonds, pistachio nuts, citrus fruits, and a host of produce. However, it is the wealth of local and artisan treasures found throughout the area that gives California its reputation as a gourmet adventure. Local creameries, cooperatives, organic gardens, gourmet chocolates, and artisan breads all add a flavor that is uniquely "California Cuisine."

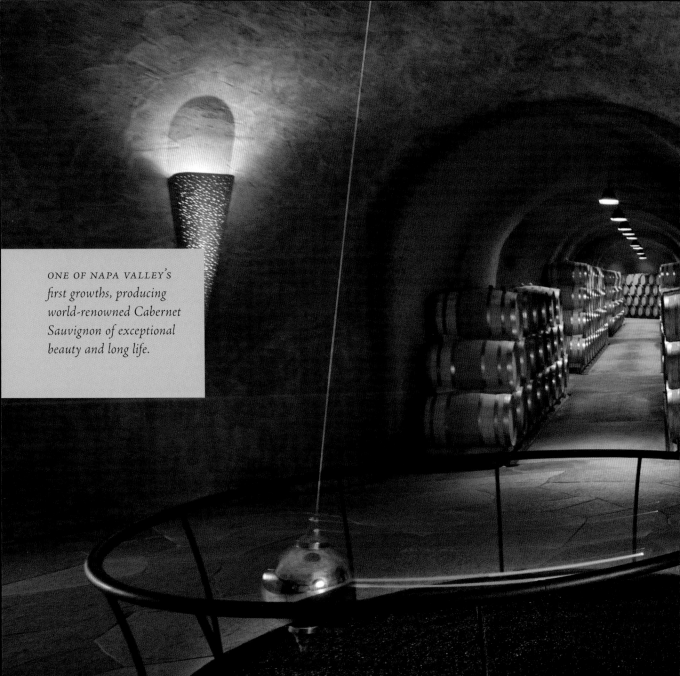

ONE OF NAPA VALLEY'S
*first growths, producing
world-renowned Cabernet
Sauvignon of exceptional
beauty and long life.*

STAG'S LEAP WINE CELLARS

S TAG'S LEAP WINE CELLARS is truly an icon of Napa Valley. I have fond memories of my visits there in the '70s, picnicking under the immense oak trees, enjoying the wines with bread, cheese, and prosciutto we bought at the Oakville Grocery. Napa Valley was mostly a local destination then.

That was before the 1976 "Judgment in Paris" put Napa Valley, and Stag's Leap Wine Cellars, on the world wine map. The Cabernet Sauvignon from the Stag's Leap Vineyard (S.L.V.) beat some of the most prestigious French wines in a blind tasting judged by French wine experts. The Napa Valley became a world-class wine destination.

Although the Napa Valley landscape has changed a lot since those early days, the quality leadership of Stag's Leap Wine Cellars' estate vineyards remains. Two of the most renowned vineyards in Napa Valley belong to Stag's Leap Wine Cellars. The Stag's Leap Vineyard (S.L.V.) yields Cabernet that is concentrated, with a spicy intensity. Adjoining S.L.V., the FAY Vineyard delivers elegant fruit with rich berry flavors. When blended together, the intense "fire"-like qualities of S.L.V. and the supple, "water"-like characteristics of FAY create the renowned Stag's Leap Wine Cellars CASK 23.

I love to create menus around CASK 23 because I can bring out the spicy "fire" qualities with bold cuts of meat and I can show the supple "water" qualities with fruit-driven reduction sauces. The complexity, power, and finesse of the wine makes a memorable meal experience.

John Sarich

STAG'S LEAP WINE CELLARS— A NAPA VALLEY FIRST-GROWTH

The story of Stag's Leap Wine Cellars and Warren Winiarski is now legendary.

After developing an appreciation for fine wine while studying in Italy, Warren made his first wine in the cramped quarters of faculty campus housing at the University of Chicago where he was a lecturer in the liberal arts. In 1964, Warren moved his family to California where he would fulfill the destiny of his family name: in Polish, "Winiarski"

ALTHOUGH STAG'S LEAP Wine Cellars S.L.V. and Fay vineyards adjoin each other, the wines they produce carry expressly different aspects of the terroir. S.L.V. soils contribute multi-layered structure, concentration, and spicy intensity, while Fay's soils yield more softness and rich berry qualities.

means "winemaker's son." In the early 1960s the Napa Valley was experiencing a renaissance and the Winiarskis were among a fresh wave of pioneers to come to the valley.

Warren searched for years to find land capable of producing wines of classic proportion and balance. He found it in 1969 when he tasted grape-growing pioneer Nathan Fay's homemade Cabernet. As luck would have it, an adjoining ranch was for sale. The Winiarski's first vineyard was planted in 1970 and named "Stag's Leap Vineyard," now known as S.L.V., after the rocky palisades jutting out from the hills above.

Warren's belief that this land could produce wines rivaling Europe's best was borne out in 1976, when Stag's Leap Wine Cellars' 1973 S.L.V. triumphed over some of France's greatest wines in a blind tasting among French wine experts in Paris. The stunning victory at what is now known as the "Judgment of Paris" established the Napa Valley as one of the world's premiere wine regions and launched Stag's Leap Wine Cellars into the ranks of the world's most noteworthy Cabernet producers.

Stag's Leap Wine Cellars is considered one of Napa Valley's first growths. Over the years, Stag's Leap Wine Cellars' wines have become some of the most highly regarded and collected wines worldwide. Winemaker Niki Pruss carries this tradition forward by fashioning wines that express classic elegance, structure, and ageability, and to reflect the place in which they are grown.

TWENTY YEARS AFTER a blind tasting sent shockwaves through the wine world, a bottle of the history-making 1973 Stag's Leap Wine Cellars' S.L.V. Cabernet Sauvignon was placed in the permanent collection of the Smithsonian's National Museum of American History.

A VISIT TO STAG'S LEAP Wine Cellars rewards guests with stunning views and extraordinary spaces. Clockwise from top: the entrance to the caves, where underground tunnels offer ideal conditions for barrel aging red wines; Only the section on an individual vine that has reached its optimum maturity level is harvested by Stag's Leap Wine Cellars; Aerial view of the S.L.V. and Fay estate vineyards.

Visiting the Estate

The winery and grounds of Stag's Leap Wine Cellars feature some of the most stunning views and extraordinary spaces in all of Napa Valley. In the center of the caves, a Foucault pendulum is suspended above the floor and gently swings to mark the passing of time, and the aging of wine. The winery's Cellarius Kitchen is a beautiful gathering place for food and wine pairing events as well as cooking demonstrations from notable guest chefs. Lending inspiration to the name and enhancing the space are two original seventeenth-century watercolors of the solar system created by the Dutch-German mathematician and cosmographer Andreas Cellarius.

Tours of the estate and wine caves are offered twice daily by appointment at (707) 261-6441 or tours@cask23.com. Visits to the Stag's Leap Wine Cellars' tasting room require no appointment for individuals or groups smaller than eight people. More information on all the tasting and tour options is available on the Stag's Leap Wine Cellars Web site at www.cask23.com.

Chef's Notes

At Stag's Leap Wine Cellars it is customary to complete the meal with artisan cheeses selected from one or more of the many local creameries, paired with complementing wines. As with wineries that dot the landscape, there are numerous small family-owned artisan cheese producers in Northern California. Exploring wine and cheese pairings is both fascinating and fun. Purchase a selection of cheeses, fruits, nuts, and quince paste from your local specialty store.

Favorite Ingredients

ALMONDS

Whole almonds add flavor and texture that complement any cheese and wine experience. California is the only state in the country that commercially produces almonds. In fact, 80 percent of the world's almonds come from California, due to an ideal climate with mild winters and dry, hot summers. Almonds are the most nutrient-dense tree nut and are widely recognized for their role in a healthy diet. Chefs favor almonds in their menus for their versatility, buttery flavor, and texture.

QUINCE PASTE

Quince is a relative of the apple and pear with honey and vanilla overtones. But it is hard, sour, and astringent in raw form so must be peeled, cored, and cooked. Quince paste is a thick jam made from the fruit, which has a sweet taste with some tartness. Quince paste is made in much the same way as applesauce or apple butter. The quince fruit is chopped and boiled in water until softened. Sugar and lemon juice are added and the mixture is pulped. The paste can be enjoyed a number of ways including spread on bread, served alongside roast meats, or alongside cheeses and nuts.

Stag's Leap Wine Cellars

Menu

APPETIZER
*Seared Scallops with
Corn and Pepper Relish*
PAGE 86

WINE
*Stag's Leap Wine Cellars
KARIA Napa Valley Chardonnay*

ENTRÉE
Braised Beef Cheeks
PAGE 188
with Roasted-Garlic Whipped Potatoes
PAGE 216

WINES
*Stag's Leap Wine Cellars
S.L.V. Estate Cabernet Sauvignon
or ARTEMIS Napa Valley
Cabernet Sauvignon*

DESSERT
*A selection of Californian
Artisanal Cheeses
(See Chef's Notes)
served with
Almonds, Figs, and Quince Paste*

WINE
*Stag's Leap Wine Cellars
ARCADIA VINEYARD Chardonnay,
Napa Valley or
CASK 23 Estate Cabernet Sauvignon,
Napa Valley*

FOUNDED IN 1973,
Conn Creek is a small
Napa Valley winery best
known for Bordeaux-
style wines

Conn Creek

I WAS INTRODUCED to Conn Creek in the late '70s when the release of its inaugural 1974 Eisele Vineyard Cabernet Sauvignon was garnering attention and praise among wine enthusiasts and critics. From there, Conn Creek quickly established itself as one of Napa Valley's top Cabernet producers. Today Conn Creek remains a small boutique Napa Valley winery focused on Cabernet Sauvignon and Bordeaux-style red wines, albeit in a much larger neighborhood.

Conn Creek is a "must" on your list of wineries to visit in the Napa Valley. Blending wine is an art, and the hands-on blending seminar offered at Conn Creek is unparalleled. Set against the backdrop of beautiful estate gardens and the Vaca Mountains, Conn Creek's unique AVA Room is a fun, educational, and memorable way to learn about the art of blending and the diversity of Napa Valley. You can taste your way through most of Napa Valley's fifteen sub-apellations. After your wine education, and the guided walk-around barrel tasting, you can then use your tasting notes to make your own personal blend to take home, complete with a custom label.

Conn Creek is ideal for passionate oenophiles looking for a sensory tour. The winery, nestled in the heart of Napa valley, is a must to include when visiting wineries on the Silverado Trail. Once you are in the care of the welcoming, attentive, and knowledgeable staff, you'll know your journey off the beaten path was greatly rewarded—their hospitality is top notch. Make sure to book an appointment and bring your camera.

JOHN SARICH

Conn Creek Winery—
A Rich Heritage of Napa Valley
Cabernet Sauvignon

Founded in 1973, Conn Creek is located on the scenic Silverado Trail in the Rutherford district of Napa Valley. Over the years, the winery discovered many exceptional single vineyard sites throughout Napa Valley, and today Conn Creek sources fruit from prized vineyards in nearly all of Napa Valley's fifteen renowned sub-appellations or AVAs.

This provides winemaker Mike McGrath with an extraordinary palette from which to blend each vintage. Like a gourmet pantry of spices, each Napa Valley sub-appellation contributes distinctive characteristics. When blended together, they create wines of generous flavors and layers of depth and complexity.

This wine-making artistry is embodied in Conn Creek's signature wine ANTHOLOGY, a beautiful and classic Bordeaux-style blend.

"THE CHARACTER OF *a wine is entrenched in the vineyard…my quest is to identify and amplify the attributes from each site.*"

MIKE MCGRATH, CONN CREEK WINEMAKER

CONN CREEK WINERY'S *AVA Room offers an immersion in Cabernet Sauvignon from Napa Valley—and a peek behind the curtain of winemaker Mike McGrath's "workshop." Barrels of Cabernet Sauvignon, each made from one of Napa Valley's sub-apellations, are organized by flavor and richness to guide guests in making their own personal blend.*

Anthology is a Greek word that refers to a collection of literary or artistic works and this wine is much the same. Like a collection of inspired words or poetry, ANTHOLOGY is made from Napa Valley's finest vineyards and diverse AVAs for growing Bordeaux-style varieties.

While each AVA contributes different characteristics to the master blend of ANTHOLOGY, they also reveal a certain beauty on their own. Each year, the winery showcases four of the most distinctive appellation wines as part of the limited production AVA Cabernet Sauvignon Series available only at the winery or through its wine club.

The Napa Valley Series of wines showcases some of the best Bordeaux-style varietals grown in this region (both red and white): a rich, full-bodied, and lively Cabernet Sauvignon; a powerful and generous Cabernet Franc; and a crisp and refreshing Sauvignon Blanc.

VISITING THE ESTATE

In its search for the best Cabernet grapes to create ANTHOLOGY, Conn Creek's AVA Room came to life. The AVA Room offers wine lovers of all levels a one-of-a-kind tasting tour of Napa Valley Cabernet Sauvignon, all in one stop. Here, guests have a rare opportunity to learn about, taste, and blend wines from the array of distinctive regions that make up Napa Valley. Best of all, guests have the opportunity to play winemaker for a day and take home a custom blended bottle of wine. The intimate two-hour AVA Room blending seminar is offered twice daily, by appointment only, Thursday through Tuesday, and can be booked on the winery's Web site at www.conncreek.com or by calling (707) 963-9100, extension 210. The Conn Creek wine shop and classic tasting room are open daily with no appointment needed.

Chef's Notes

With Conn Creek's focus on classic Napa Valley Cabernet Sauvignon and Bordeaux-style red wines, a favored pairing to show the depth of the wine's flavor is a beef dish featuring stuffing made of pancetta, olives, Asiago cheese, and olive oil.

FAVORITE INGREDIENTS

AVOCADOS
Although there are close to five hundred varieties of avocados, seven varieties are grown commercially in California. Haas is the most popular. California's seven thousand avocado groves produce about 90 percent of the nation's avocado crop. Avocados are actually a fruit and not a vegetable.

OLIVES
Seventy to eighty percent of all ripe olives grown in America are grown in California. The olive was introduced to California in the late-eighteenth century by Spanish missionaries who planted olive trees at each of the twenty-one missions they established between San Diego and Sonoma.

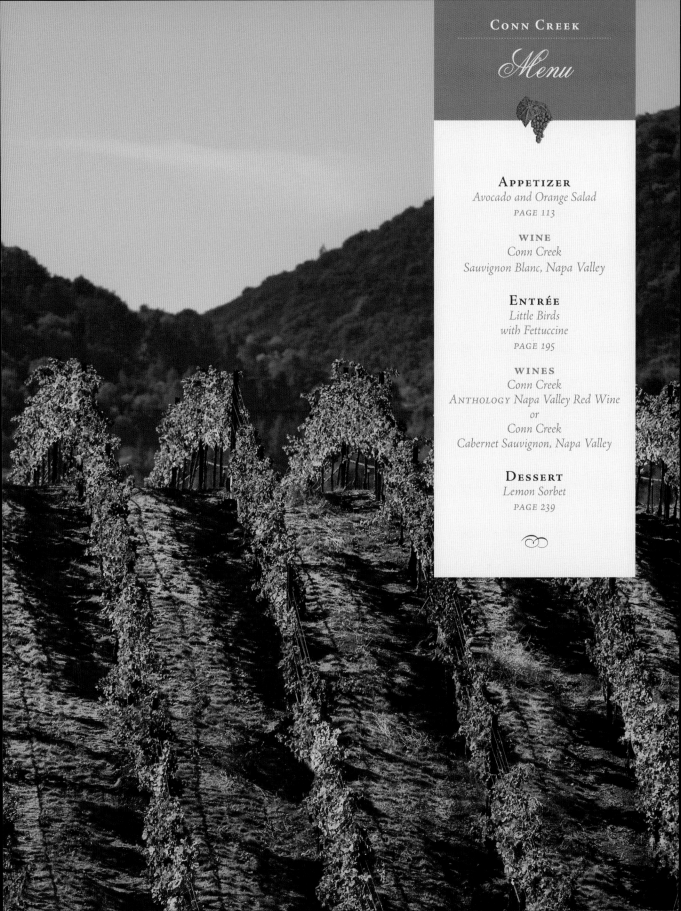

CONN CREEK

Menu

APPETIZER
Avocado and Orange Salad
PAGE 113

WINE
*Conn Creek
Sauvignon Blanc, Napa Valley*

ENTRÉE
*Little Birds
with Fettuccine*
PAGE 195

WINES
Conn Creek
ANTHOLOGY *Napa Valley Red Wine*
or
*Conn Creek
Cabernet Sauvignon, Napa Valley*

DESSERT
Lemon Sorbet
PAGE 239

ANTICA IS A SYMBOL *for Antinori California and represents the realization of a long-standing desire to produce great Antinori family wines in Napa Valley*

Antica

NAPA VALLEY

THERE ARE MANY factors that influence the flavors of wine: terroir, soil, climate, temperature, altitude, and wine-making styles. For me, the one ingredient that makes wine so special is the romance around it. Where you had that special bottle, with whom you had it, and what you had to eat with it, all add to the experience.

Having a Mediterranean background, I am especially fond of the Antinori wines, both in Italy and here in the United States. Marchese Piero Antinori—who prompted a revolution in Italian wine by blending his native Sangiovese with small amounts of Cabernet Sauvignon in the creation of Tignanello—is one of the most influential winemakers of our time.

Antica is a symbol for Antinori California, the Antinori Family wine estate in Napa Valley. It is a Napa Valley experience like no other. The beauty of the mountainside estate is unparalleled with its views, expanse of vineyards, caves, and charming winery. But what makes this estate so unique is the history behind it from one the oldest and most esteemed wine-making families in Italy.

The Antinori Family has been making wine for over six hundred years. The family has personally managed the business throughout its long history, and the business continues to be entirely family owned. Through twenty-six generations, the Antinori Family have established a reputation for its innovative, courageous choices, high-regard for tradition, and unwavering respect for the land.

I had the honor and the pleasure of cooking for the Marchese and his daughters Alessia, Allegra. and Albiera, who are all involved in the family business. Their passion for exploring and pushing the boundaries in order to learn and grow is an inspiration to every winemaker, chef, connoisseur, and food lover in America.

JOHN SARICH

ANTICA NAPA VALLEY

Piero Antinori visited Napa Valley for the first time in the 1960s and fell in love with the area. Although his home and family wine-making history have been rooted in Tuscany for over six hundred years, he was driven to learn and understand what was taking place in the New World. Piero Antinori returned to Napa Valley in the 1980s when he and other business partners discovered this beautiful

"Ancient roots play an important role in our philosophy, but they have never held back our spirit of innovation."

MARCHESE
PIERO ANTINORI

1,200-acre wine estate. In the 1990s their increasing certainty of the potential of this terroir led the Antinori Family to make a personal investment and assume direct one hundred percent ownership of the vineyard and winery. Today the winery is Antica—which is the symbol for Antinori California.

Antica is located in the remote Atlas Peak District at 1,500–2,000 feet above sea level in the eastern mountains of Napa Valley. Its hilly terrain, rocky soils, high elevations, and beautiful landscape create an estate ideal for winegrowing.

The Antica estate vineyard is planted to Cabernet Sauvignon and Chardonnay—the two most important grape varieties grown in the Napa Valley. The wine's powerful character comes from the grapes grown in the New World, but the wine's finesse and elegance come from the Antinori experience as an Old World wine producer.

In September 2007, limited quantities of the much anticipated inaugural vintages of Antica Napa Valley Cabernet Sauvignon and Chardonnay were released.

"I would say we achieved what we were hoping for in the wines of Antica," says Alessia Antinori, one of Piero Antinori's three daughters who is deeply involved in carrying on the family's legacy. "We have brought together the best of both wine worlds and made a wine that has both power and elegance. For me and my family, to have our name on the bottle is a big responsibility because each bottle of wine has more than six hundred years of wine-making history behind it. It is a challenge we accept gracefully as we must preserve what our ancestors have accomplished while looking forward and being open-minded to what lies ahead for our children and future generations."

ENTRANCE TO THE ANTICA Napa Valley wine caves which are carved into the granite mountainside. The conditions inside the caves provide ideal aging for the wines.

VISITING ANTICA NAPA VALLEY

The Antica Napa Valley estate rewards guests with breath-taking views and an elegant tasting experience. Sitting atop one of the highest points in Napa Valley, the panorama one can take in while strolling the grounds includes an expanse of estate vineyards, wine caves carved into the granite mountainside, and views to the southwest through the valley to the tip of the San Francisco Bay Bridge. Antica Napa Valley is less than a two-hour drive from San Francisco and is located just northeast of the city of Napa. Guests are welcomed by appointment only, which can be made by calling the winery or through the Web site at www.anticanapavalley.com.

If you plan to visit, consider a stay in the quaint town of Yountville. This small, historic town is centrally located in the valley and boasts many bed and breakfasts, inns, and outstanding restaurants.

Chef's Notes

Stuzzichini (Italian for appetizers), which are most often found in the Enotecas, or Italian wine bars, are often served at Antica Napa Valley. They are simple to make, pair well with wine, and are based on the seasonal produce available from the estate and the local market.

Chef Kim Wiss has shared some recipes that reflect Antica's Tuscan heritage and pair wonderfully with Antica Napa Valley Cabernet Sauvignon and Chardonnay.

At Antica Napa Valley, often a meal is finished with a cheese course to enjoy while sipping Antica Napa Valley Cabernet Sauvignon. The apricot and fig fruit preserves that are served with this menu's Italian cheese course provide just the right touch of sweetness to satisfy those wanting to finish their meal with that sensory pleasure.

FAVORITE INGREDIENTS

FIGS

About a half dozen fig varieties are commercially grown in California, including Calimyrna, Mission, Kadota, and Adriatic. The Napa Valley's Black Mission Fig takes its name from the Franciscan fathers who planted this variety. The all-too-brief season of this nutritious fruit begins in June and culminates in October.

FRUITS AND NUTS

In addition to wine grapes, the Antinori Family's Antica Napa Valley estate grows various varieties of fruits and nuts. The mountainside estate has a small orchard where apricot, fig, apple, Italian plum, orange, peach, and walnut trees grow. Throughout the property many olive trees grow among the grapevines. Antica Napa Valley produces its own olive oil from these estate olives.

ANTICA NAPA VALLEY

Menu

BY CHEF KIM WISS

APPETIZER
*Anchovy Butter with Sun-dried
Tomatoes and Parsley Sauce*
PAGE 89

*Bruschetta with Ricotta, Spring Peas,
Pancetta, and Mint*
PAGE 90

Eggplant Agrodolce (Caponata)
PAGE 93

*Italian Cheese Course featuring
Apricot Preserves and Fig Preserves*
PAGE 96

Robiola Cheese Sandwiches
PAGE 102

*Sautéed Carciofi
with Fresh Burrata*
PAGE 103

Sautéed Cavolo Nero on Crostini
PAGE 104

*Smoked Salmon
with Arugula Sauce on Crostini*
PAGE 105

*Schiacciata
(Fall Harvest Grape Cake with Fennel)*
PAGE 245

WINES
*Antica Napa Valley
Cabernet Sauvignon
or Chardonnay*

Continuing the Journey

THERE IS AN ART to food and wine pairing. It is an art learned through experimentation over a span of time. If you are new to the study of pairing wine with food then you have an enjoyable journey ahead.

As you strive to master that art yourself, let the guidelines for wine pairing presented in *Chef in the Vineyard* coach you through the exploration. You are going to find that your overall culinary experience is enhanced when you find the perfect combination of flavors.

For those of you who have ventured far into acquiring the skill of matching your food and beverage, then I hope this book will open up new pleasures. I love sharing my personal journey through these distinctive vineyards. Some of these wineries are fresh and original, and others are steeped in tradition; all of them share an unshakeable passion for wine making. The visual journey presented here brings you closer to the land, which is the source of all good wine. Yet, there is nothing as good as standing on that land where the grapes are grown, or walking through the state-of-the-art facilities where great wines are made. It is my wish that you will someday travel to visit these wineries for yourself.

The Recipes

I am sure that as you browse the pages of this book you will find just the meals you have been seeking, whether you are looking for recipes for a family banquet, a lively dinner party, a romantic occasion, a weekend picnic, or weeknight supper. Remember,

some meals you cook at home may be better suited to a cold beer or a glass of water with a squeeze of lemon. In my opinion, your dessert may be better without any wine at all—a good-quality coffee drink might be the very thing.

So, pour yourself a glass of wine, make yourself a little finger food, and drift off to the vineyards in your mind. May your armchair travel through these incredible wineries inspire you to cook great meals for your friends and family.

Wine Temperature

The temperature of wine is as important as what food to serve with it. Most white wines, except Rieslings, sparking wines, and dessert wines are best served at about 50°F; your refrigerator is at least 40°F, if not colder. The flavor and bouquet of the wine is masked when it is too cold. To raise the temperature, it is important to take white wine out of the refrigerator twenty minutes before serving.

Red wines should not be consumed at room temperature but at cellar temperature, which is about 60°-64°F. When red wine is served too warm, the tannins, acids, and alcohol tastes are too pronounced. If the red wine is stored at room temperature, put it in the refrigerator for about twenty minutes to chill it down a little before serving.

❧ Appetizers ❧

Asian Dungeness Crab Cocktail

I prefer to use Dungeness crab from the Pacific Northwest, but fresh and locally grown are more important than the variety of crab.

1 pound fresh crabmeat

1 small red bell pepper, diced

4 green onions, diced

⅛ cup julienned jicama

1 clove garlic, chopped

⅛ teaspoon peeled grated fresh ginger

1 tablespoon chopped fresh cilantro

1 teaspoon rice vinegar

1 teaspoon sesame oil

Toss the crabmeat together with the other ingredients until the crabmeat is completely coated. Serve in a martini glass or on a plate of lettuce leaves.

WINE
RECOMMENDATIONS:

CHATEAU STE. MICHELLE
& DR. LOOSEN
*Eroica Riesling,
Columbia Valley*

CHATEAU STE. MICHELLE
*Gewürztraminer,
Columbia Valley*

GRILLED PEACHES WITH PROSCIUTTO

Warm, flavorful, grilled peaches make a simple first course. In inclement weather they can be cooked inside under the broiler.

4 ripe peaches, halved crosswise, skins on   ⅓ pound sliced prosciutto
1 tablespoon olive oil   4 slices fresh bread

Preheat an outdoor grill on medium heat.

Brush the cut-side of each peach with the oil. Place the peaches on the grill over medium heat, cut-side down. Place the bread slices on the grill and turn the bread over once grill marks develop, about 1 to 2 minutes each side. Remove the bread from the grill when toasted to a golden brown on both sides. Continue to grill the peaches until marks develop, about 3 to 5 minutes. Remove the peaches from the grill.

Place the peaches on a plate and top with the slices of prosciutto. Serve the grilled bread on the side.

WINE
RECOMMENDATIONS:

COLUMBIA CREST
*Two Vines
Sauvignon Blanc,
Columbia Valley*

DOMAINE STE. MICHELLE
*Brut Sparkling Wine,
Columbia Valley*

Seared Scallops with Corn and Pepper Relish

Sweet and spicy peppers make a colorful pairing with the sweetness of summer corn.

2 tablespoons olive oil	½ cup chicken broth
4 large sea scallops	2 tablespoons cream
½ teaspoon salt	3 ears corn, cooked, kernels removed, divided
2 cloves garlic, chopped	Pinch cayenne pepper
1 small red bell pepper, diced	Fresh cilantro
⅛ cup diced roasted green chiles	

Heat the olive oil in a sauté pan on medium-high heat. Add the scallops to the hot oil; lightly salt them. Sauté the scallops on both sides until browned, about 2 to 3 minutes per side. Remove scallops from pan.

Add the garlic, red bell pepper, and chiles; sauté until soft.

Blend the chicken broth, cream, half the corn, and cayenne pepper in a blender or food processor until smooth. Season with salt to taste.

Add the sautéed vegetables and the other half of the corn to the mixture in the blender; stir until well combined.

To serve, spoon equal portions of the relish onto four small plates. Top each plate of corn with a scallop. Garnish with a fresh cilantro sprig, or freshly chopped cilantro if preferred.

Wine
Recommendations:

Stag's Leap Wine Cellars
Karia Napa Valley Chardonnay
or
Napa Valley Sauvignon Blanc

AHI POKE

Try this piquant salad made from raw ahi tuna. It is a popular Hawaiian dish that is fresh, flavorful, and satisfying; it is local Hawaiian comfort food.

¾ pound raw ahi tuna
¼ cup soy sauce
1 teaspoon rice vinegar
½ teaspoon peanut oil
1 teaspoon sesame oil
½ teaspoon chopped fresh ginger
½ teaspoon chopped garlic

Juice of ½ lime
Pinch sugar
½ teaspoon nori flakes
3 green onions, finely chopped
1 tablespoon sesame seeds, for garnish
1 teaspoon chopped fresh cilantro, for garnish

Cut the ahi tuna into bite-size pieces. Place the ahi tuna and all remaining ingredients in a medium bowl and toss together gently, until the tuna is completely coated. Chill. This can be made ahead of time and marinated for 1 hour.

Garnish with the sesame seeds and cilantro.

WINE
RECOMMENDATIONS:

COLUMBIA CREST
*Grand Estates Sauvignon Blanc,
Columbia Valley*

ERATH
Oregon Pinot Noir

Anchovy Butter with Sun-dried Tomatoes and Parsley Sauce

Chef Kim Wiss, Antica Napa Valley

2 cloves garlic

1 bunch Italian parsley

Pinch salt

Pinch black pepper

1 cup unsalted butter, room
temperature

1 (3½-ounce) can anchovies, oil
packed, drained

4 sun-dried tomatoes, packed in olive
oil, drained, cut into thirds

12 miniature rolls about 2 inches in
diameter, or 12 crostini

Place the garlic and parsley in a food processor and process until smooth.
Add salt and pepper to taste. Transfer to a small dish. Clean the food processor so
it can be used to make the anchovy butter.

Place the softened butter and anchovies in a clean food processor. Process
until smooth.

Slice the rolls, and spread each with 1 spoonful of the anchovy butter. Add 1
sun-dried tomato and drizzle a little of the parsley sauce on top of the tomato.

*This is a nice little
sandwich that offers a
lot of flavor and is easy
to prepare. It is based on
the traditional anchovy
sandwiches served at
the Antinori's Procacci
restaurant in Florence.*

WINE
RECOMMENDATIONS:

ANTICA NAPA VALLEY
Chardonnay

ERATH
Oregon Pinot Gris

BRUSCHETTA WITH RICOTTA, SPRING PEAS, PANCETTA, AND MINT

CHEF KIM WISS, ANTICA NAPA VALLEY

Bruschetta is similar to topped crostini, except that the bread is larger in size, and grilled on both sides—usually over coals on a grill. The grilled bread is then an empty canvas waiting for you to place whatever you prefer on top. It is a great way to use leftovers and what is in season; use your imagination. At the winery, we use ciabatta bread to make the bruschetta.

2 tablespoons olive oil

4 ounces pancetta, cut into ¼-inch pieces

6 ounces fresh peas, blanched

4 mint leaves, sliced into thin strips

Salt, to taste

Black pepper, to taste

8 ounces fresh ricotta

8 slices ciabatta bread, grilled on both sides

Heat the olive oil in a sauté pan. Add the cubed pancetta to the hot oil and cook until crispy, being careful not to burn it. Add the blanched peas, sauté for 2 minutes, and add salt and pepper to taste.

Place ricotta in a small bowl and season with salt and pepper to taste.

Place approximately 2 tablespoons of the ricotta on each slice of the ciabatta bread. Top with a sprinkling of pancetta, the fresh peas, and a little more olive oil. Sprinkle some of the mint onto each bruschetta.

Serve immediately.

OTHER VARIATIONS:

+Add a mixture of chopped tomatoes and basil, and top with grilled shrimp.

+Place 3 slices of bresaola on each bruschetta, add a slice of Fontina and place under the broiler to melt the cheese. Top with a slice of pear.

WINE RECOMMENDATIONS:

ANTICA NAPA VALLEY
Chardonnay
OR
Cabernet Sauvignon

CHICKEN LIVER PÂTÉ ON CROSTINI

2 tablespoons butter

4 shallots, finely chopped

2 cloves garlic, chopped

2 pounds chicken livers

½ cup finely chopped mushrooms

⅛ cup Sauvignon Blanc

1 teaspoon sherry vinegar

Pinch cayenne pepper

Dash truffle oil

Salt, to taste

White pepper, to taste

Crostini, for serving

Heat the butter in a large skillet on medium-high heat. Sauté the shallots and garlic until soft, about 5 minutes. Add the chicken livers and mushrooms. Continue to sauté them, stirring frequently, until golden brown, about 6 minutes. Stir in the wine and vinegar. Season with the cayenne pepper, truffle oil, salt, and white pepper to taste. Cook, stirring frequently, for 5 minutes. Cool.

Blend the cooled liver mixture in a food processor until smooth.

Spread on crostini and serve.

Process this quickly and you have a coarsely textured spread similar to a country pâté. To achieve a smooth and spreadable texture, process the spread until it reaches a satiny consistency.

WINE
RECOMMENDATIONS:

SHINING HILL
*Red Wine,
Columbia Valley*

CHATEAU STE. MICHELLE
*Sauvignon Blanc,
Columbia Valley*

CROATIAN CALAMARI

When shopping for squid, look for ones that are small-sized and clear-eyed. Squid becomes rubbery if overcooked, so keep the grilling time short.

8 large squid, cleaned

2 cloves garlic, chopped

¼ cup olive oil

1 teaspoon chopped fresh basil

1 teaspoon chopped fresh Italian parsley

⅛ cup Sauvignon Blanc

Juice of ½ lemon

Pinch salt

Pinch black pepper

Preheat an outdoor grill on hot heat.

Toss the squid together with the other ingredients until the squid is completely coated. Let stand about 15 minutes.

Grill the squid on both sides over hot coals, about 4 minutes per side.

Eggplant Agrodolce (Caponata)

Chef Kim Wiss, Antica Napa Valley

⅛ cup olive oil, for frying

1 large Italian eggplant or 4 Japanese eggplants (no salting needed), sliced into ¼-inch diagonal slices

1 small red onion, diced into ½-inch pieces.

3 tablespoons tomato paste

1 cup water

3 tablespoons flavored honey

6 ounces red or white wine vinegar

2 tablespoons capers, packed in brine, with the juice

3 Italian parsley leaves, chopped

Salt, to taste

Black pepper, to taste

¼ cup grated Parmesan cheese

If using Italian eggplant, cube and salt the eggplant and allow to sit for 30 minutes. Rinse, drain and dry with a towel to remove any remaining moisture.

Heat the olive oil in a non-stick frying pan. When hot, add the sliced eggplant, and fry until golden brown. Avoid crowding the pan. Do not allow the eggplant to burn. When golden, remove the eggplant from the pan, and drain on a paper towel.

Using the same sauté pan, add approximately 2 tablespoons of the olive oil if there is none remaining in the pan. Sauté onions until they begin to sweat and take on color. Add the honey and vinegar and allow to reduce for approximately 1 minute.

Add the tomato paste and water; stir. Return the eggplant to the pan and allow to simmer for approximately 5 more minutes.

Remove from the heat and stir in the capers and parsley. Add salt and pepper to taste. Sprinkle cheese on top.

I love eggplant and love the sweet and sour taste of this dish. We usually leave it in a bowl and top with either a soft cheese like Burrata or ricotta or a harder grating cheese like Parmigiano-Reggiano for that added saltiness, and allow guests to serve themselves. I use Italian parsley to add a touch of freshness to the dish, but you can also substitute fresh mint or basil. You can also adjust the honey or vinegar depending on your preference. Serve with grilled bread.

Wine Recommendations:

Antica Napa Valley
Chardonnay
or
Cabernet Sauvignon

FAVA BEAN DIP MALTESE-STYLE

The unmistakable flavor of fresh fava beans is captured in this dip. Fava beans, available fresh in the spring, are popular in Mediterranean and Middle Eastern dishes. Serve this dip in a bowl surrounded with pita bread, and sprinkled with freshly chopped Italian parsley.

1½ pounds fresh fava beans (unshelled), to yield about 1½ cups
3 cloves garlic, mashed
1 tablespoon lemon juice
⅛ teaspoon hot paprika
⅛ teaspoon ground cumin

Pinch salt
Pinch pepper
¼ cup extra virgin olive oil, plus extra if needed
Chopped fresh Italian parsley, for garnish

Shell the beans. Bring water to a boil in a medium saucepan. Add the beans and decrease heat. Simmer to release the outer waxy covering on the beans, about 3 minutes. Drain, rinse with cold water, and remove the outer skin.

Hand-mash the cooked beans with all other ingredients or, preferably, blend all ingredients in a food processor or blender until smooth. Season with additional spices, salt, and pepper to taste. More olive oil may be added to achieve desired consistency. Garnish the dip with parsley.

WINE
RECOMMENDATIONS:

COLUMBIA CREST
Grand Estates Pinot Grigio,
Columbia Valley

ERATH
Willamette Valley Pinot Blanc

FRIED RAZOR CLAMS

1½ cups flour

1 teaspoon paprika

Pinch chopped fresh thyme

Pinch salt

½ teaspoon white pepper

1 pint razor clams, shucked

1 tablespoon olive oil

1 tablespoon butter

2 cloves garlic, mashed

2 tablespoons Sauvignon Blanc

1 teaspoon lemon juice

Mix the flour, paprika, thyme, salt, and white pepper in a shallow dish. Dredge the clams in the seasoned flour mixture and set aside.

Heat the olive oil and butter in a large skillet on medium-high heat. Sauté the garlic until light brown, about 2 minutes. Add the floured clams and cook until brown on both sides, about 2 minutes per side. Remove the clams from the pan and place on a serving dish.

Make the sauce by adding the wine and lemon juice to the pan, stirring to loosen the browned bits from the bottom. Bring to a boil. Remove from heat.

Pour sauce over clams and serve.

The razor clam is a popular soft-shell clam from the West Coast. The most commonly available soft-shell clam on the East Coast is the steamer clam. Cook these gently to keep them tender.

WINE
RECOMMENDATIONS:

ERATH
Oregon Pinot Gris

COLUMBIA CREST
Two Vines Sauvignon Blanc, Columbia Valley

Fruit Preserves
for Italian Cheese Course

Chef Kim Wiss, Antica Napa Valley

When entertaining, you can never go wrong with serving cheese. At Antica Napa Valley, we like to finish a meal with a cheese course as it pairs well with Antica Napa Valley Cabernet Sauvignon and the fruit provides that touch of sweetness that everyone seems to crave after a wonderful meal. Of course, we often just serve a selection of cheeses to accompany a wine tasting.

FOR CHEESE BOARD:

3 to 5 diverse hard and soft artisanal cheeses and Italian cheeses

FOR APRICOT PRESERVES:

8½ ounces granulated sugar

3 pounds apricots, pits removed, chopped into very large pieces, saving all juice

½ teaspoon cardamom seeds

Canning jars, sterilized according to manufacturer's directions

Place the sugar in a large heavy-gauge saucepan and bring to simmer. In essence, you will be making a very light caramel sauce. Once the sugar is melted and simmering, add the apricots and any collected juice and stir with a wooden spoon.

The apricots will continue to release juice as they break down and simmer. Continue to simmer until the preserves appear thick, approximately 1 hour. Stir in the cardamom seeds.

Using a small chilled plate, place ½ teaspoon of the hot mixture on the plate to test for doneness. If the preserves run down the plate when it is tilted, continue cooking the mixture. If it does not run, the preserves are ready to can.

Following the manufacturer's directions for water-bath canning, fill each hot, sterile jar to the fill line; seal jars. Cover with boiling water in a large pot. Boil for 15 minutes. Remove from water and allow to cool; refrigerate.

WINE RECOMMENDATIONS:

ANTICA NAPA VALLEY
Chardonnay
OR
Cabernet Sauvignon

FIG PRESERVES

9½ ounces granulated sugar

3 pounds fresh figs, cleaned and
   de-stemmed

½ teaspoon cardamom seeds

Canning jars, sterilized according to
   manufacturer's directions

Put the sugar in a large heavy-gauge saucepan and bring to simmer. In essence, you will be making a very light caramel sauce. Once the sugar is melted and simmering, add the figs and any collected juice and stir with a wooden spoon.

The figs will continue to release juice as they break down and simmer. Continue to simmer until the preserves appear thick, approximately 1 hour. Stir in the cardamom seeds.

Using a small chilled plate, place ½ teaspoon of the hot mixture on the plate to test for doneness. If the preserves run down the plate when it is tilted, continue cooking the mixture. If it does not run, the preserves are ready to can.

Following the manufacturer's directions for water-bath canning, fill each hot, sterile jar to the fill line; seal jars. Cover with boiling water in a large pot. Boil for 15 minutes. Remove from water and allow to cool; refrigerate.

MOZZARELLA, TOMATO, AND PROSCIUTTO SKEWERS

These colorful, flavorful skewers make a quick and easy appetizer. They can also be served on their own, because as fun as it is to cook up a meal to match with your favorite wine, sometimes all you really need to enjoy your wine is a loaf of crusty French bread, fresh tomatoes, basil, prosciutto, cheese, and of course great company.

FOR SKEWERS:

12 small cherry tomatoes

12 small fresh mozzarella balls

12 basil leaves

12 pieces of prosciutto cut into 2-inch squares

12 small skewers

FOR DRESSING:

½ cup olive oil

¼ cup balsamic vinegar

1 teaspoon dry mustard

1 clove garlic, chopped

TO PREPARE SKEWERS: Thread tomatoes, mozzarella balls, basil leaves, and prosciutto squares onto skewers, alternating to have 3 of each per skewer.

TO PREPARE DRESSING: Whisk together all the dressing ingredients. Drizzle the dressing over the kebabs and serve.

WINE
RECOMMENDATION:

DOMAINE STE. MICHELLE
*Brut Sparkling Wine,
Columbia Valley*

Nori Rice Cakes with Sweet Orange-Ginger Sauce

FOR SWEET ORANGE-GINGER SAUCE:

⅓ cup soy sauce

1 tablespoon rice vinegar

Juice of ½ orange

1 tablespoon peanut oil

¼ teaspoon sesame oil

½ teaspoon peeled chopped fresh ginger

2 cloves garlic, mashed

1 tablespoon honey

1 tablespoon chopped fresh cilantro

FOR NORI RICE CAKES:

1 cup sushi (short grain) rice (to make 2 cups cooked)

1 large egg

⅔ cup soy sauce

4 green onions, finely chopped

½ to 1 teaspoon nori flakes

2 tablespoons peanut or vegetable oil, for frying

TO PREPARE SAUCE: Blend all ingredients in a blender or food processor until smooth.

TO PREPARE RICE CAKES: Bring rice and 2 cups water to a boil. Reduce to simmer and cook, covered, until tender, about 15 minutes. Let cool.

Whisk egg with soy sauce in a large bowl. Add rice and remaining ingredients to the egg mixture and mix well. Form mixture into 8 patties, measuring about 3-inches in diameter and about 1-inch thick.

Heat oil in a sauté pan. Add rice cakes and brown well, about 2 minutes per side.

Nori, dried seaweed, is available in the Asian section of most grocery stores or from local Asian markets. This recipe makes eight rice cakes and will serve four people as an appetizer. The sauce adds incredible flavor when served on the plates along with the Nori Rice Cakes.

WINE RECOMMENDATIONS:

CHATEAU STE. MICHELLE
Riesling,
Columbia Valley
SNOQUALMIE
Naked Gewürztraminer,
Columbia Valley

OLIVE TAPENADE

1 cup pitted Greek black olives
¼ cup roasted red peppers
4 anchovy fillets
1 tablespoon capers
3 cloves garlic, mashed
1 tablespoon coarsely chopped fresh oregano

1 tablespoon coarsely chopped fresh Italian parsley
1 teaspoon dry mustard
½ teaspoon ground cumin
2 tablespoons balsamic vinegar
French bread, for serving

Blend all ingredients together in a food processor until smooth. Refrigerate 1 hour. Serve in a bowl surrounded with French bread slices.

PROSCIUTTO-WRAPPED STUFFED DATES

12 large pitted dates
5 ounces Gorgonzola cheese

6 slices prosciutto, halved lengthwise
Olive oil

Preheat the oven to 350°F.
Stuff each date with Gorgonzola. Wrap a half-slice of the prosciutto around each date. Brush a baking sheet with olive oil. Place the dates on the sheet and bake in the oven for 3 minutes.

Risotto Cakes with Goat Cheese and Mushrooms

FOR RISOTTO:

1 quart (4 cups) chicken stock

1 tablespoon olive oil

1 tablespoon butter

1 small yellow onion, diced

1 small red bell pepper, diced

2 cloves garlic

½ teaspoon finely chopped fresh thyme

1 teaspoon Dijon mustard

1 cup sliced fresh mushrooms (chanterelle or porcini)

⅛ cup Chardonnay

1 cup Arborio rice

FOR RISOTTO CAKES:

1 recipe Risotto (see above)

6 ounces goat cheese

⅛ cup cream

¼ cup fine dry bread crumbs

1 tablespoon butter

1 tablespoon olive oil

½ cup veal or chicken stock

FOR SERVING:

Arugula or spinach leaves

Fresh thyme

Freshly grated Parmesan cheese

These risotto cakes can be prepared and breaded up to two hours ahead; then they only require a few minutes to brown and plate before serving. This recipe makes about eight small risotto cakes. As for the wine, Sauvignon Blanc and goat cheese are a heavenly match.

TO PREPARE RISOTTO: Bring the chicken stock to a boil in a covered saucepan. Reduce the heat to low; cover and continue to simmer until needed.

Heat the oil and butter in a heavy saucepan on medium heat. Sauté the onion, pepper, and garlic until very soft, about 4 to 6 minutes. Stir in the thyme, mustard, mushrooms, wine, and rice. Cook over medium-high heat, stirring, until the rice absorbs liquid, about 2 minutes. Using a ladle, slowly add simmering stock 1 ladle at a time. Stir and boil for 2 minutes. Reduce the heat to low; cover, and cook until the rice is tender, about 20 minutes. Cool.

TO PREPARE RISOTTO CAKES: Mix the goat cheese and cream into the cooled rice. Use only enough cream to moisten and form the rice mixture into patties. Pat into eight hockey-puck-size portions. Roll the cakes in the bread crumbs.

When ready to serve, heat a sauté pan to medium-high heat and add the butter and oil. Brown the risotto cakes on both sides.

TO SERVE: Place the risotto cakes in serving bowl and pour the stock around the cakes. Garnish with the arugula or spinach, thyme, and Parmesan cheese.

WINE RECOMMENDATIONS:

CHATEAU STE. MICHELLE
*Chardonnay,
Columbia Valley*

COLUMBIA CREST
*Grand Estates Sauvignon Blanc,
Columbia Valley*

Robiola Cheese Sandwiches

Chef Kim Wiss, Antica Napa Valley

At the winery, we always like to serve something little to go along with our wine tastings, and these match perfectly with our Antica Chardonnay. This recipe makes twelve to sixteen biscuits depending on the size of the cookie cutter used. It is best to serve them warm from the oven so that the cheese begins to soften in the sandwich. Robiola cheese can usually be found in either a fresh form or a more savory form. Either will work in this recipe.

Wine
Recommendation:

Antica Napa Valley
Chardonnay

1¾ cup flour

2 teaspoons baking powder

¼ cup grated Parmesan cheese

2 teaspoons dried rosemary or sage, or both, depending on your preference

1 teaspoon salt (more can be added)

4 tablespoons cold unsalted butter, cut into small dice

2 tablespoons extra virgin olive oil

1 egg

⅓ cup milk

2 tablespoons cream

8 ounces Robiola cheese

Combine the flour, baking powder, Parmesan cheese, dried herbs, and salt in a bowl. Add the butter, and using your fingers, work the butter into the flour mixture. The finished product should look like small peas. In a separate bowl, combine the oil, egg, and milk, and then add to the flour mixture. Working quickly, stir the mixture until it resembles a ball. Now is a good time to taste the dough and test for salt; add more if needed. Place the biscotti dough on a lightly floured surface and bring together using your hands. Do not overwork the dough.

Place the dough in the refrigerator for approximately 20 minutes to allow the flavors to marry and rest the dough.

Preheat the oven to 375°F.

Remove the biscotti from the refrigerator, and using a rolling pin, roll to a thickness of ⅓ inch. Using a cutter, cut the dough into desired shape and place on a parchment lined sheet pan. Using a pastry brush, gently brush the tops of each biscuit with the cream.

Place in preheated oven, and bake until golden, approximately 20 minutes. Do not overbake.

While the biscuits are baking, slice the Robiola into nice wedges or slices that will fit into your biscuit.

Remove the biscuits from the oven. Slice open and place a piece of cheese inside. Serve warm.

Note: The biscotti can be stored in an airtight container for up to 2 days.

Sautéed Carciofi (Artichokes) with Fresh Burrata

Chef Kim Wiss, Antica Napa Valley

Juice of 2 lemons, divided
10 baby (2-pounds) artichokes
¼ cup olive oil
½ red onion, chopped
½ cup Chardonnay
½ cup chicken stock
1 sprig fresh thyme

2 tablespoons chopped fresh parsley
Salt, to taste
Black pepper, to taste
1 baguette, sliced into 18 crostini
Olive oil, for drizzling
1 whole clove garlic
4 ounces Burrata cheese

Put 2 quarts of water in a non-reactive bowl. Squeeze the juice of 1 lemon in the water.

Working with 1 artichoke at a time, trim the outer leaves until you reach the pale leaves. Cut off the top of the artichoke—close to the top of the heart section. Trim the stem of the artichoke, about ¼ inch. Peel the stem, removing the outer layer of toughness. Cut the artichokes into quarters, removing any choke that is mature, as it will not cook and will remain tough. Place the artichoke quarters in the acidulated water. Repeat with the remaining artichokes.

Heat the olive oil in a medium saucepan. Add the chopped red onion. Dry and drain the artichokes and add to the saucepan. Toss the artichokes in olive oil until they begin to take on a little golden color.

Add the wine, being careful of splatters. Reduce for 3 minutes, and add the chicken stock and thyme sprig. Continue to braise the artichokes until tender, adding additional stock if needed. When the artichokes are tender, add the juice of remaining lemon and the parsley. Toss and season with salt and pepper to taste.

Preheat the broiler. Toast the baguette slices under the broiler, until golden brown. Remove from the oven and rub with olive oil and garlic while still warm.

Place artichokes with their sauce in a large bowl-shaped platter. Crumble the Burrata on top. Season with additional salt and pepper for flavor, and drizzle with olive oil. Serve the artichokes with the crostini.

In the spring, when artichokes are in season, we serve baby artichokes with fresh Burrata cheese.

Burrata is similar to buffalo mozzarella, with the addition of cream in the center of the cheese ball. Serve this recipe on a plate with crostini, and allow your guests to serve themselves, or place on individual crostini and serve as an appetizer.

Wine Recommendation:

Antica Napa Valley
Chardonnay

SAUTÉED CAVOLO NERO ON CROSTINI

CHEF KIM WISS, ANTICA NAPA VALLEY

After finishing culinary school, I spent three months working at two famous Florentine restaurants: Buca Lapi and Procacci. This dish was featured on the menu at Buca Lapi, and I have adjusted to suit the American palate. At the winery we serve this as an appetizer, but it can also be served as an accompaniment to beef and pork entrées. It is easier to find kale in the fall and winter months.

Use crostini for this dish—thin slices of baguette, toasted in the oven until golden. Traditionally, it is only toasted on one side. Rub a little olive oil on each crostini before toasting.

3 large bunches Cavolo Nero (black kale, dinosaur kale)	Salt, to taste
¼ cup olive oil	Black pepper, to taste
2 cloves garlic, chopped, divided	12 crostini
	Grated Parmigiano-Reggiano

Boil water in a large stockpot.

Wash the kale, and remove the leaves from the stems. The best way to do this is to hold the kale stem in one hand, and pinching the leaf between the thumb and finger of your other hand, strip it away from the stem. Once the water is boiling, put the kale leaves in the water with a very large pinch of salt. This will help keep the leaves green. Allow the kale to boil for approximately 10 minutes. Drain, and squeeze the water from the leaves. Chop the dried kale.

Heat the olive oil in a sauté pan.

Add the kale to the heated olive oil, along with half the garlic. Sauté until tender, approximately 5 minutes. Add additional olive oil if needed.

When the kale is tender, add the remaining chopped garlic. Season with salt and pepper to taste.

While hot, place 1 large tablespoon of the sautéed kale on each crostini, and drizzle with additional olive oil. Sprinkle grated Parmigiano-Reggiano on top for additional flavor. Serve immediately.

SMOKED SALMON WITH ARUGULA SAUCE ON CROSTINI

CHEF KIM WISS, ANTICA NAPA VALLEY

3 bunches arugula, stems removed

Juice of 1 lemon

Salt, to taste

Black pepper, to taste

1 container (8-ounces) cream cheese

16 miniature rolls or fresh sliced
baguette (not toasted)

4 ounces smoked salmon, sliced into
16 pieces

Place the arugula in a food processor with the lemon juice. Pulse until blended. Add salt and pepper to taste. Add the cream cheese and continue to pulse. Adjust seasonings with more salt and pepper. More lemon juice can also be added at this time.

Cut open the rolls and spread a little of the arugula sauce on each roll. Top with a slice of smoked salmon.

This is a dish based on a recipe I learned to make at the Antinori Family's Procacci restaurant in Florence, Italy. The enoteca is famous for serving little sandwiches that pair well with all of their Italian wines. This recipe pairs well with the Antica Napa Valley Chardonnay and offers a lot of flavor to complement the wine.

WINE
RECOMMENDATIONS:

ANTICA NAPA VALLEY
Chardonnay

CHATEAU STE. MICHELLE
*Cold Creek Vineyard Riesling,
Columbia Valley*

STEAMED CLAMS

Clams are a high-protein shellfish with fair amounts of calcium and iron. Hard-shell or soft-shell clams can be used for this flavorful dish made from fresh, basic ingredients.

2 pounds clams
2 cloves garlic, mashed
2 tablespoons olive oil
Juice of ½ lemon
¼ cup Sauvignon Blanc
1 teaspoon chopped rosemary

1 teaspoon chopped Italian parsley
Pinch red pepper flakes
12 cherry tomatoes, halved
1 tablespoon chopped fresh basil, for garnish

Place the clams in a large pot with a lid. Add all the other ingredients except the basil. Cover and steam the clams over high heat shaking the pot occasionally until the clams open, about 5 minutes.

Place onto a serving dish and garnish with the chopped basil.

WINE RECOMMENDATIONS:

CHATEAU STE. MICHELLE
Pinot Gris,
Columbia Valley

SNOQUALMIE
Sauvignon Blanc,
Columbia Valley

❦ Soups & Salads ❧

Asian Crab Noodle Soup

*There's nothing like soup
to warm your spirits.*

2 cloves garlic, thinly sliced

1 tablespoon grated or thinly sliced
fresh ginger

1 tablespoon peanut oil

½ teaspoon sesame oil

1 teaspoon Vietnamese fish sauce,
(optional)

1 teaspoon soy sauce, or to taste

6 cups chicken, vegetable, or seafood
stock

1 pound vermicelli or thin Asian rice
noodles

1 tablespoon chopped fresh cilantro

1 tablespoon chopped fresh basil

1 tablespoon chopped fresh mint

1 bunch green onions, sliced thin on
diagonal

1 pound cooked fresh Dungeness or
king crab

Chili oil or chili paste, to taste
(optional)

Sauté the garlic and ginger in the peanut and sesame oils in a 6-quart sauce-pan, over medium heat, just until lightly softened. Add the fish sauce, soy sauce, and stock. Bring to a low boil. Add the noodles. Cook until the noodles are just tender, about 5 to 7 minutes. Stir in the cilantro, basil, mint, and green onions.

Ladle into serving bowls and top with the fresh crab. Add the chili oil or paste if desired.

Wine
Recommendations:

Chateau Ste. Michelle
& Dr. Loosen
*Eroica Riesling,
Columbia Valley*

Columbia Crest
*Two Vines Gewürztraminer,
Columbia Valley*

BEAN AND CHICKEN SOUP WITH GREENS

1 stewing chicken or small whole fryer

1 tablespoon olive oil

2 onions, finely chopped

2 cloves garlic, finely chopped

1 cup Roma tomatoes, chopped

1 bunch endive or escarole, cleaned and coarsely chopped

4 cups chicken stock

¼ cup Sauvignon Blanc

1 (15-ounce) can white beans (cannellini, Great Northern, or navy)

Salt, to taste

Parmesan cheese, for garnish

Fresh basil, for garnish

Freshly ground black pepper

Bring the chicken to a boil in a large stockpot; reduce heat, cover, and simmer until cooked through, about 1 to 1¼ hours. Remove the chicken; cool, and take the meat off the bones.

Heat olive oil and sauté onions and garlic until soft in a large soup pot. Add tomatoes and sauté until just soft. Add chopped endive or escarole and sauté until wilted. Stir in chicken stock and wine. Bring to a slow boil. Add beans and chicken meat and simmer 15 minutes. Season with salt to taste.

Ladle into bowls. Sprinkle with Parmesan cheese and garnish with fresh basil. Top with freshly ground pepper to finish.

A soup made of common ingredients may be construed as boring, but deep down we all know that bean and chicken soup satisfies both the stomach and the soul.

WINE RECOMMENDATIONS:

STAG'S LEAP WINE CELLARS
Napa Valley Sauvignon Blanc

COLUMBIA CREST
*H3 Chardonnay,
Horse Heaven Hills*

OR

*Two Vines Shiraz,
Columbia Valley*

Djani's Pasta e Fagiole

We pronounce this "pasta fagool." A hearty dish like this is tremendous served with a generous amount of Parmesan cheese, a tossed green salad of arugula dressed with an oil and vinegar dressing, good crusty bread, and olives. Although there is white wine in the dish, the finished recipe works well with a red wine.

2 cups small white beans or navy beans
1 medium smoked ham hock
¼ cup olive oil
2 yellow onions, diced small
2 tablespoons chopped pancetta or bacon
1 small sweet yellow bell pepper, diced
2 small yellow potatoes, diced
6 cloves garlic, chopped
½ cup chopped fresh Italian parsley
3 or 4 sprigs fresh thyme

1 bay leaf
Pinch freshly grated nutmeg
⅛ teaspoon paprika
Pinch cayenne pepper
½ cup dry white wine
1 quart chicken broth
1 cup ziti pasta, elbows, or other small pasta
Salt, to taste
Black pepper, to taste
Parmesan cheese, for garnish

Soak beans overnight in water, or in a pan of water bring the beans to a boil then remove from heat and let stand 1 hour.

Place ham hock in a large stockpot and cover with water. Bring to a boil. Reduce heat and simmer, covered, for about 1 hour or until meet falls from the bone. Remove from the pot. Pull the meat apart and reserve.

Heat olive oil in a large skillet. Sauté onions and pancetta in the oil until soft. Add peppers and sauté 5 more minutes. Add potatoes and continue to cook. Chop together parsley and garlic until very fine and add to the cooking vegetables. Add thyme sprigs, bay leaf, nutmeg, paprika, cayenne pepper. Stir in wine and 1 cup of the chicken broth. Simmer 15 minutes. Add beans, the meat from the ham hock, and another cup of stock. Cover and simmer until beans begin to soften, stirring occasionally and adding more stock as necessary. Add pasta and cook until pasta and beans are soft, adding more stock as needed. This should be a thick soup or stew consistency. Season with salt and pepper to taste. Serve with Parmesan cheese.

LENTIL SOUP

⅛ cup olive oil

1 cup chopped red bell peppers

1 cup chopped yellow bell peppers

2 cups chopped onions

2 bunches Swiss chard, chopped

4 cloves garlic, chopped

1 bulb fresh fennel, chopped

3 cups lentils

6 cups chicken broth

1 cup Cabernet Sauvignon

2 tablespoon chopped fresh oregano

1 tablespoon chopped fresh Italian
 parsley

1 teaspoon ground cumin

Pinch red pepper flakes

½ teaspoon salt, or to taste

¼ teaspoon black pepper, or to taste

Heat olive oil in a heavy stockpot. Sauté vegetables in olive oil until soft. Add all other ingredients and simmer for 2 hours, stirring occasionally. Season with salt and pepper to taste.

Can a meal get much healthier than this? Perhaps it can, if you serve whole-wheat bread along with it. The color of the lentils is up to you— brown, red, or a combination.

WINE
RECOMMENDATIONS:

COLUMBIA CREST
*H3 Cabernet Sauvignon,
Horse Heaven Hills*

OR

*Two Vines Merlot-Cabernet,
Columbia Valley*

CHATEAU STE. MICHELLE
*Merlot,
Columbia Valley*

SPRING VALLEY VINEYARD
*Uriah Red Wine,
Walla Walla Valley*

TUGBOAT SHELLFISH CHOWDER WITH PISTOU

Serve with grilled garlic bread and top with a spoonful of pistou, which is basically pesto with herbs.

FOR CHOWDER:

⅛ cup pancetta, chopped (optional)

2 tablespoons olive oil

4 small red potatoes, diced

1 small fennel bulb, chopped

1 large onion, chopped

1 red bell pepper, chopped

3 cloves garlic, chopped

¼ cup celery, chopped

2 cups chopped Roma tomatoes or 1 (14-ounce) can ready-cut tomatoes in purée

½ cup Sauvignon Blanc

¼ teaspoon dry mustard

1 bay leaf

2 sprigs thyme

Pinch salt

Pinch white pepper

FOR SHELLFISH:

1½ pounds clams

1½ pounds mussels

FOR PISTOU:

1 cup basil leaves

½ cup Italian parsley

¼ cup tarragon leaves

2 tablespoons thyme

½ cup olive oil

3 cloves garlic

¼ teaspoon salt

TO PREPARE CHOWDER: Heat oil in a large sauté pan over medium-high heat. Sauté pancetta and all the vegetables in oil until soft, about 10 minutes. Add tomatoes, wine, dry mustard, bay leaf, thyme, salt, and pepper. Simmer for 10 minutes.

TO PREPARE SHELLFISH: Add clams and mussels to the vegetables. Cover and simmer just until the shells open.

TO PREPARE PISTOU: Place all ingredients in a food processor and blend until smooth.

TO SERVE: Ladle the chowder into serving bowls and top with the pistou.

WINE RECOMMENDATIONS:

STAG'S LEAP WINE CELLARS
Napa Valley Sauvignon Blanc

CHATEAU STE. MICHELLE
*Syrah,
Columbia Valley*

Avocado and Orange Salad

FOR DRESSING:

¼ cup olive oil

Juice of ½ lemon

Juice of 1 lime

2 cloves garlic, mashed

½ teaspoon dry mustard

¼ teaspoon chili powder

¼ teaspoon honey

Pinch salt

Pinch black pepper

FOR SALAD:

2 heads Bibb lettuce

1 large avocado, cut into thin wedges

2 tomatoes, cut into wedges

1 to 2 oranges, peeled and cut into
   segments

1 red onion, cut into thin slices

1 tablespoon chopped fresh cilantro,
   for garnish

TO PREPARE DRESSING: Place all the dressing ingredients into a jar and shake well, or blend in a blender until smooth.

TO PREPARE SALAD: Place the lettuce on a plate. Arrange the prepared avocado, tomatoes, oranges, and onion on top of the lettuce. Garnish with the cilantro.

TO SERVE: Drizzle the salad with the dressing just before serving.

For avocado lovers—this colorful, flavorful, and satisfying salad is a refreshing way to enjoy avocado.

WINE RECOMMENDATIONS:

Conn Creeek
Sauvignon Blanc,
Napa Valley

Stag's Leap Wine Cellars
Arcadia Vineyard
Chardonnay,
Napa Valley

Chicken and Creamy Tarragon Salad

If you love fresh asparagus as much as I do then you are sure to appreciate the delicious simplicity of this beautifully arranged dinner salad.

FOR TARRAGON DRESSING:

½ cup chopped fresh tarragon leaves
¼ cup chopped fresh Italian parsley
2 cloves garlic, chopped
⅛ cup olive oil
1½ tablespoons white wine vinegar
1 tablespoon Dijon mustard

1 tablespoon capers
⅛ cup mayonnaise
⅛ teaspoon paprika
Pinch of sugar
Pinch salt

FOR CHICKEN:

1 whole fryer chicken (roasted and
   meat removed from bones)
1 head romaine lettuce
3 cups mixed field greens

2 tomatoes, cut into wedges
1 red onion, thinly sliced
12 asparagus spears, blanched

TO PREPARE DRESSING: Purée the tarragon, parsley, garlic, and olive oil in a blender or food processor until smooth. Add the vinegar, mustard, capers, mayonnaise, paprika, sugar, and salt and blend or process thoroughly.

TO PREPARE SALAD: Preheat the oven to 350°F.

Roast chicken in preheated oven for 1½ hours, until cooked through. Remove meat from bones; shred. Store chicken in refrigerator until ready to use.

Arrange whole romaine leaves in a star fashion on a chilled plate. Toss the field greens with a little tarragon dressing and place in the center of the leaves. Place shredded chicken meat on top of greens. Arrange tomato and asparagus around the salad. Place red onion slices on top of salad. Drizzle more dressing over the entire salad.

WINE
RECOMMENDATION:

CHATEAU STE. MICHELLE
*Indian Wells Chardonnay,
Columbia Valley*

CHILLED CHICKEN AND VEGETABLE SALAD

1½ cups julienned cooked chicken strips

2 tomatoes, quartered

1 small red onion, thinly sliced

½ cucumber, thinly sliced

1 red bell pepper, thinly sliced

1 clove garlic, chopped

1 tablespoon chopped fresh oregano

1 tablespoon chopped fresh Italian parsley

½ cup croutons

⅛ cup red wine vinegar

¼ cup extra virgin olive oil

Pinch of sugar

Pinch salt

Pinch black

10 romaine lettuce leaves

Toss together chicken, tomatoes, red onion, cucumber, red bell pepper, garlic, oregano, Italian parsley, croutons, red wine vinegar, olive oil, sugar, salt, and pepper and let stand about 20 minutes. Line a salad bowl with romaine lettuce and place salad mixture on top.

Beef, lamb, or pork may be substituted for the chicken. This is a complete meal that is fresh and healthy.

WINE RECOMMENDATIONS:

CHATEAU STE. MICHELLE
Indian Wells Chardonnay, Columbia Valley

OR

Dry Riesling, Columbia Valley

HEIRLOOM TOMATO SALAD

When heirlooms are not in season you can still make this with any vine-ripened tomatoes. Simple to prepare using staple ingredients—but the taste is divine.

FOR DRESSING:

1 tablespoons red wine vinegar

1 tablespoon balsamic vinegar

4 tablespoons extra virgin olive oil

1 clove garlic, mashed

½ teaspoon dry mustard

Pinch sugar

Pinch salt

Freshly ground black pepper

FOR SALAD:

4 mixed-variety heirloom tomatoes, sliced into rounds

1 red onion, sliced into thin rings

Fresh basil, thinly sliced into ribbons (about 2 tablespoons), for garnish

TO PREPARE DRESSING: Mix the red wine vinegar, balsamic vinegar, olive oil, garlic, mustard, sugar, salt, and black pepper in a small jar. Shake until emulsified.

TO PREPARE SALAD: Stack the tomatoes and onions on a platter. Garnish with basil.

TO SERVE: Drizzle dressing over the salad.

WINE
RECOMMENDATION:

SNOQUALMIE
*Naked Riesling,
Columbia Valley*

SUMMER SALAD NIÇOISE WITH GRILLED ASPARAGUS

The tuna and asparagus are grilled on a hot outdoor grill. They can also be seared in a sauté pan on top of the stove. Don't limit yourself to the vegetable ingredients listed, you may add just about any veggie that strikes your fancy.

WINE
RECOMMENDATIONS:

ERATH
Oregon Pinot Noir

SNOQUALMIE
*Sauvignon Blanc,
Columbia Valley*

COLUMBIA CREST
*Two Vines Vineyard 10 Rose,
Columbia Valley*

FOR DRESSING:

2 tablespoons olive oil

Juice of 1 lemon

1 tablespoon Dijon mustard

1 garlic clove, chopped

1 teaspoon chopped fresh basil
  or tarragon

1 teaspoon chopped capers

2 anchovy fillets chopped (optional)

½ teaspoon sugar

Pinch salt

Pinch white pepper

FOR SALAD:

4 cups mixed field greens

2 tomatoes, cut into wedges

1/2 cup sliced green beans

1 small red onion, thinly sliced

Greek black olives

2 hard-boiled eggs, quartered

FOR TUNA AND ASPARAGUS:

2 (1-inch thick) tuna fillets (6- to 8-
  ounces each)

1 pound asparagus, ends snapped off

1 garlic clove, mashed

¼ cup olive oil, divided

 Salt

Freshly ground black pepper

TO PREPARE DRESSING: Place all the ingredients in a jar and shake until blended.

TO PREPARE SALAD: Place the mixed greens on a large plate. Place the tomato wedges, green beans, sliced red onions, olives, and eggs on top.

TO PREPARE TUNA AND ASPARAGUS: Preheat an outdoor grill on hot heat.

Rub the tuna fillets with garlic; pour and rub on some of the olive oil. Season with salt and pepper to taste.

In a separate dish, toss the asparagus with some olive oil, salt, and pepper.

Place the tuna and asparagus on hot grill. Sear the tuna about 1½ minutes per side. Grill the asparagus until just tender.

TO SERVE: Place the asparagus spears on top of the salad. Slice the tuna thinly and arrange on top. Drizzle the dressing over the salad.

COLD STEAK SALAD

This could just as easily be named "Pepper, Onion, and Tomato Salad." You can serve this as a main meal, or perhaps accompanied by a pasta or risotto side dish for a heartier meal. For variety, try flat iron steak or change the cheese to Gorgonzola.

1 pound flank steak
1 red bell pepper, sliced
1 yellow bell pepper, sliced
1 green bell pepper, sliced
1 large Walla Walla Sweet Onion, sliced
2 cloves garlic, chopped
2 cups Roma tomatoes, cut into wedges
2 tablespoons freshly chopped oregano
2 tablespoons freshly chopped Italian parsley
Pinch salt

Pinch black pepper
Pinch pepper flakes
½ cup virgin olive oil
¼ cup red wine vinegar
2 tablespoons balsamic vinegar
1 teaspoon dry mustard
1 head romaine lettuce, coarsely chopped
⅛ cup Romano or Pecorino cheese, coarsely grated, for garnish
12 whole green olives (optional)

To grill steak, preheat an outdoor grill to hot. Place the steak on the grill and cook to medium-rare, turning only once, about 9 to 10 minutes per side.

To broil steak, preheat the broiler. Place the steak on a broiling pan and broil 2 to 3 inches from heat, for about 7 minutes per side.

Slice the steak into thin slices, cutting across the grain. Toss ingredients from steak to dry mustard together until thoroughly combined. Let stand for 30 minutes. Serve over crisp chilled romaine lettuce. Garnish with cheese. Add whole green olives if desired.

WINE
RECOMMENDATIONS:

CHATEAU STE. MICHELLE
Cold Creek Vineyard
Cabernet Sauvignon,
Columbia Valley

COLUMBIA CREST
Grand Estates Merlot,
Columbia Valley

COL SOLARE
Red Wine,
Columbia Valley

DUNGENESS CRAB SALAD

FOR DRESSING:

1 small red pepper, finely diced

1 garlic clove, mashed

½ teaspoon peeled grated ginger

1 teaspoon chopped fresh cilantro

1 teaspoon lime juice

½ teaspoon rice vinegar

½ teaspoon peanut oil

¼ teaspoon sesame oil

FOR CRAB SALAD:

½ pound fresh Dungeness crabmeat

Lettuce leaves, such as endive, radic-
chio, or butter lettuce

TO PREPARE DRESSING: Mix all dressing ingredients in a medium bowl.

TO PREPARE CRAB SALAD: Toss the crabmeat together with the dressing until
the crabmeat is completely coated. Arrange the lettuce on a plate and place the
crab salad on top of the lettuce.

*Serve this as a salad or
an appetizer. Substitute
the Dungeness crabmeat
with your local crab or
any other crabmeat that
you prefer.*

WINE
RECOMMENDATIONS:

CHATEAU STE. MICHELLE
*Horse Heaven Vineyard
Sauvignon Blanc,
Horse Heaven Hills*

OR

*Cold Creek Vineyard Riesling,
Columbia Valley*

LEO'S GREEK SALAD

Crisp cucumber, crumbly cheese, and juicy tomatoes combine to create a lively country salad.

FOR DRESSING:

¼ cup red wine vinegar

½ cup olive oil

1 clove garlic, chopped

Pinch sugar

Pinch salt

Pinch pepper

FOR SALAD:

1 red bell pepper, thinly sliced

1 green bell pepper, thinly sliced

1 red onion, thinly sliced

2 tomatoes, diced

1 English cucumber, sliced or cubed

4 ounces (¼ pound) crumbled feta cheese

½ cup Greek black olives

2 tablespoons chopped fresh basil

2 tablespoons chopped fresh oregano

2 tablespoons chopped fresh Italian parsley

FOR SERVING:

2 heads hearts of romaine

TO PREPARE DRESSING: Mix all the ingredients together in a large bowl.

TO PREPARE SALAD: Toss all the vegetables, cheese, olives, and herbs together with the dressing until completely coated.

TO SERVE: Arrange the hearts of romaine on a platter. Place the salad on top of the lettuce.

WINE RECOMMENDATIONS:

SNOQUALMIE
*Naked Gewürztraminer,
Columbia Valley*
OR
*Naked Riesling,
Columbia Valley*

Napa Salad

FOR DRESSING:

¼ cup Chardonnay

¼ cup extra virgin olive oil

1 shallot, finely chopped

1 teaspoon Dijon mustard

1 teaspoon chopped fresh tarragon

Pinch sugar

Pinch salt

Pinch black pepper

FOR SALAD:

4 cups mixed field greens

⅓ cup julienned jicama

⅓ cup julienned cucumber

1 red tomato, cut into wedges

1 yellow tomato, cut into wedges

1 green tomato, cut into wedges

⅛ cup dried cherries (optional)

4 green onions, cut into thin strips

TO PREPARE DRESSING: Heat the wine in a small saucepan over medium heat until reduced by half. Set aside to cool.

Blend all the dressing ingredients together, including the wine reduction, in a food processor or blender, or shake together in a jar.

TO PREPARE SALAD: Toss the ingredients together in a large serving bowl.

TO SERVE: Pour the dressing over the salad mixture and lightly toss until coated.

You'll need to make the dressing for this salad ahead of time as the Chardonnay reduction needs time to cool. For a quicker option, substitute the juice from half a lemon for the Chardonnay.

WINE
RECOMMENDATION:

STAG'S LEAP WINE CELLARS
*KARIA Napa Valley
Chardonnay*

Prosciutto Salad Rolls

Salty prosciutto is offset by fresh greens to make a fancy little side dish.

FOR DRESSING:

⅓ cup balsamic vinegar

⅔ cup extra virgin olive oil

1 clove garlic, mashed

1 teaspoon Dijon mustard

Splash Worcestershire sauce

Pinch salt

Pinch pepper

Pinch sugar

Squeeze of lemon juice

FOR SALAD:

8 thin slices prosciutto

3 cups mixed fresh greens

½ cup sliced dried figs

¼ cup pine nuts

Fresh goat cheese

TO PREPARE DRESSING: Place all the ingredients in a jar and shake vigorously.

TO PREPARE SALAD: Overlap 2 pieces of the prosciutto. Place the greens in the middle of the prosciutto and roll up together. Do this to make 4 rolls. Place on plates and garnish with portions of the figs, pine nuts, and goat cheese.

TO SERVE: Drizzle the rolls with the dressing.

WINE
RECOMMENDATIONS:

ERATH
Oregon Pinot Gris

CHATEAU STE. MICHELLE
*Horse Heaven Vineyard
Sauvignon Blanc,
Horse Heaven Hills*

ROASTED SWEET PEPPER SALAD

FOR PEPPERS:

2 red bell peppers, sliced medium
  julienne

2 yellow bell peppers, sliced medium
  julienne

6 cloves garlic, halved

⅓ cup olive oil

1 tablespoon dried oregano

½ teaspoon sea salt

FOR DRESSING:

1 large white onion, thinly sliced

2 tablespoons chopped fresh Italian
  parsley

2 tablespoons chopped fresh basil

⅓ cup olive oil

¼ cup balsamic vinegar

TO PREPARE PEPPERS: Preheat oven to 350°F.

Toss together all ingredients. Place on a baking sheet and bake in preheated oven for 30 minutes, turning frequently, until soft and slightly browned.

Remove from oven and cool.

TO PREPARE DRESSING: Mix together all dressing ingredients.

TO SERVE: Toss roasted peppers with dressing. Refrigerate for 1 hour or serve at room temperature.

Crumbled goat cheese makes a nice addition to this colorful salad.

Sweet Onion and Tomato Salad

Many varieties of mild, sweet onions can be used including Maui, Vidalia, and Walla Walla. Look for onions that are locally grown or in season and combine them with fresh tomatoes.

WINE
RECOMMENDATION:

CHATEAU STE. MICHELLE
*Sauvignon Blanc,
Columbia Valley*

1 clove garlic, mashed
2 tablespoons chopped fresh basil
¼ teaspoon dry mustard
2 tablespoons balsamic vinegar
2 tablespoons extra virgin olive oil
Pinch sugar

Pinch salt
Freshly ground black pepper
3 small sweet onions, sliced into
  rounds
4 medium tomatoes, cut into wedges

Blend or thoroughly mix the garlic, basil, mustard, vinegar, olive oil, sugar, salt, and black pepper in a medium bowl. Toss the onions and tomatoes gently with the dressing. Let stand at room temperature for 30 minutes before serving.

Tabbouleh Salad

A generous amount of parsley is a must in this traditional salad.

WINE
RECOMMENDATION:

COLUMBIA CREST
*Two Vines Riesling,
Columbia Valley*

4 cups cooked bulghur wheat
2 to 3 cups parsley, chopped
4 Roma tomatoes, chopped
6 green onions, chopped
⅛ cup fresh mint, chopped

2 cloves garlic, finely chopped
Juice of 1½ lemons
⅛ cup extra virgin olive oil
Pinch salt

Mix all ingredients together thoroughly. Refrigerate for ½ hour to allow flavors to mix.

Warm Potato Salad

FOR DRESSING:

⅛ cup red wine vinegar

¼ cup extra virgin olive oil

⅛ teaspoon sugar

Pinch salt

Pinch black pepper

FOR VEGETABLES:

8 medium red potatoes, quartered

½ pound green beans

2 cloves garlic

2 cups baby arugula

1 cup halved baby Roma tomatoes

⅛ teaspoon chopped fresh basil

TO PREPARE DRESSING: Place all the ingredients in a jar and shake until mixed thoroughly.

TO PREPARE POTATOES: Boil the potatoes in salted water in a saucepan until almost done. Add the garlic and beans. Cook until the potatoes and beans are tender; drain. Toss the potatoes and beans with the arugula, tomatoes, and basil.

TO SERVE: Pour the dressing over the warm vegetables and toss until the vegetables are completely coated.

Not just your ordinary potato salad! The addition of garden vegetables puts a spin on a classic summer side dish.

WINE
RECOMMENDATIONS:

SNOQUALMIE
*Naked Chardonnay,
Columbia Valley*

OR

*Two Vines Vineyard 10 Rose,
Columbia Valley*

White Bean and Roasted Garlic Salad

Begin this wonderful salad a day ahead of time, as the flavor is enhanced when the ingredients mingle for twelve to twenty-four hours before serving. This versatile side dish can also be a main dish for another occasion, just add some lettuce and poached chicken or fish.

Wine Recommendations:

Stag's Leap Wine Cellars
*Arcadia Vineyard
Chardonnay,
Napa Valley*

Snoqualmie
*Syrah,
Columbia Valley*

FOR ROASTED GARLIC:

2 heads garlic

1 tablespoon olive oil

FOR BEAN SALAD:

2 (15 ounce) cans white beans, drained and rinsed

1 (14 ounce) can hearts of palm, sliced into ½ inch thick pieces

¼ cup thinly sliced fresh sage

¼ cup lemon juice

⅓ cup extra virgin olive oil

½ teaspoon salt

¼ teaspoon ground white pepper

TO PREPARE ROASTED GARLIC: Preheat the oven to 375°F. Using clean hands, rub the garlic heads lightly with 1 tablespoon of the olive oil and wrap loosely in foil. Bake until the garlic head gives a bit with a gentle squeeze, about 35 to 40 minutes. Cool the roasted garlic until comfortable to handle. Using a serrated knife, slice off the root end to expose the large ends of the garlic cloves. Using both hands, squeeze from the sprout end toward the root to extract the cloves. The cloves should easily slide out if the garlic has been cooked properly and is still slightly warm. Roasted garlic may be stored in the refrigerator in a sealed container for up to 1 week.

TO PREPARE BEAN SALAD: Twelve to twenty-four hours before serving, mix the garlic, beans, hearts of palm, sage, lemon juice, olive oil, salt, and pepper together in a large bowl.

TO STORE AND SERVE: Refrigerate in the serving bowl, covered with plastic wrap. Remove the salad from the refrigerator 1 hour before serving. Serve at room temperature.

∾ SEAFOOD ∾

Avocado and Prawn Burrito

A folded and rolled
flour tortilla can enclose
so many savory fillings,
there's no need to limit the
options to beans,
rice, and cheese. This
exceptional combination
still retains the Mexican
flair that comes from
chili powder, cilantro, and
jalapeño pepper.

FOR AVOCADO AND PRAWN FILLING:

½ pound large prawns, shelled and cooked

2 small avocados, diced

1 small red onion, diced

2 cloves garlic, finely chopped

3 Roma tomatoes, chopped

Juice of 1 lime

¼ teaspoon chili powder

Pinch cumin

1 tablespoon chopped fresh cilantro

1 tablespoon olive oil

1 jalapeño pepper, diced

Pinch salt

FOR SALSA:

2 cups chopped Roma tomatoes

¼ cup chopped green onions

⅛ cup extra virgin olive oil

1 tablespoon balsamic vinegar

2 tablespoons red wine vinegar

2 tablespoons chopped fresh basil

2 tablespoons chopped fresh Italian parsley

2 tablespoons chopped Greek olives

Pinch pepper flakes

Pinch sugar

Pinch salt

Pinch black pepper

FOR SERVING:

6 flour tortillas

TO PREPARE FILLING: Cut the prawns in half lengthwise. Mix the prawns and all the remaining ingredients for the filling in a medium bowl; do not mash the avocado.

TO PREPARE SALSA: Mix all ingredients and let stand for 1 hour.

Process salsa quickly in a blender or food processor; do not over-process, salsa should remain slightly chunky.

TO SERVE: Cut each tortilla in half. Roll each half tortilla into a cone. Fill the tortillas with the mixture. Serve with the salsa.

Wine Recommendations:

Stag's Leap Wine Cellars
Napa Valley
Sauvignon Blanc

Chateau Ste. Michelle
Riesling,
Columbia Valley

Erath
Oregon Pinot Gris

BAKED CRAB-STUFFED AVOCADO

2 avocados cut in half lengthwise with
  meat removed (leave skin intact for
  stuffing)
1 cup Dungeness crabmeat
½ cup mayonnaise
2 tablespoons horseradish

Juice of ½ lemon
⅛ teaspoon paprika
½ teaspoon chopped fresh tarragon
Pinch salt
Pinch of red pepper flakes

Preheat the oven to 350°F.

Stir avocado and all other stuffing ingredients together until well combined.
Stuff halves of avocado skins with mixture.

Bake in preheated oven for 20 minutes.

You've found the perfect solution if you've been searching for something to serve for an elegant brunch. Don't let this suggestion limit you though; it's also incredible as an appetizer for a holiday dinner.

WINE
RECOMMENDATIONS:

CHATEAU STE. MICHELLE
Dry Riesling,
Columbia Valley

STAG'S LEAP WINE CELLARS
KARIA Napa Valley
Chardonnay

Clam Bake Pasta

A terrific way to serve pasta is with steamer clams or razor clams; you could even substitute mussels for this dish. Serve over pasta as a main course, or serve the clams by themselves as an appetizer.

FOR CLAMS:

1½ pounds soft-shell clams

1 to 2 cloves garlic, chopped

1 shallot, chopped

1 tablespoon olive oil

1 to 2 Roma tomatoes, chopped

1 tablespoon chopped fresh basil

¼ cup Chardonnay or Sauvignon Blanc

FOR PASTA:

1 pound pasta (spaghetti, vermicelli, or linguine)

FOR GARNISH:

Fresh chopped Italian parsley, for garnish

TO PREPARE CLAMS: Place all the ingredients into a heavy skillet or large saucepan. Cover and steam over medium-high heat, shaking occasionally until the clams open, about 5 to 7 minutes.

TO PREPARE PASTA: Boil water in a large stockpot. Add the pasta and cook according to package directions, or until al dente. Drain the pasta and place on a serving platter.

TO SERVE: Pour the clams and their sauce over the pasta and garnish with parsley.

WINE
RECOMMENDATIONS:

COLUMBIA CREST
*Two Vines Chardonnay,
Columbia Valley*

CHATEAU STE. MICHELLE
*Pinot Gris,
Columbia Valley*

CRAB CAPPELLINI

FOR CRAB SAUCE:

1 tablespoon butter

1 tablespoon olive oil

1 large onion, thinly julienned

1 small fennel bulb, thinly julienned

2 cloves garlic, mashed

1½ cups chopped Roma tomatoes

½ cup chicken stock

¼ cup Chardonnay

½ cup cream

Pinch saffron threads

Pinch lemon zest

⅓ cup Parmesan cheese

3 tablespoons chopped fresh basil

¾ pound fresh crabmeat

FOR PASTA:

1 pound cappellini or angel hair pasta

TO PREPARE CRAB SAUCE: Heat the butter and olive oil in a high-sided large sauté pan. Sauté the onion, fennel, and garlic until very soft, about 10 minutes. Add the tomatoes and simmer another 5 minutes. Add the stock and wine and simmer 5 minutes more. Add the cream, saffron, and lemon zest. Simmer until thickened. Stir in the Parmesan cheese, then add the basil and crabmeat.

TO PREPARE PASTA: Bring water to a boil in a large stock pot. Place the pasta into boiling water and cook al dente, about 6 to 8 minutes or according to package directions. Drain the pasta. Pour the crab sauce over the pasta to serve.

Fresh crabmeat is showcased in this recipe. Instead of the standard seafood in cream sauce dish that appears on many restaurant menus, this creamy pasta dish is improved with wine, saffron, and basil.

WINE
RECOMMENDATIONS:

CHATEAU STE. MICHELLE
*Canoe Ridge
Estate Chardonnay,
Horse Heaven Hills*
OR
*Cold Creek Vineyard Riesling,
Columbia Valley*

CRAB SCRAMBLE WITH
LAVENDER CREAM CHEESE AND BAGELS

The cream cheese can be mixed ahead and stored in the refrigerator. Bring it to room temperature before spreading it on the bagels.

FOR CRAB SCRAMBLE:

4 large eggs, with splash of water
Dash of Tabasco sauce
½ teaspoon grated ginger (optional)
1 teaspoon chopped fresh tarragon
Pinch salt

Pinch white pepper
1 tablespoon butter
2 large shallots, thinly sliced
½ cup grape or cherry tomatoes, halved
½ pound fresh crabmeat

FOR LAVENDER CREAM CHEESE:

1 (16-ounce) container whipped cream
  cheese
1 tablespoon honey

1 teaspoon grated orange zest
½ teaspoon chopped fresh lavender

FOR SERVING:

4 bagels

TO PREPARE CRAB SCRAMBLE: Beat or whisk the eggs with a splash of water in a medium bowl. Add the Tabasco sauce, ginger, tarragon, salt, and white pepper.

Heat the butter and sauté the shallots until tender in a large nonstick skillet. Add the tomatoes and increase heat to high. Pour in the eggs; be careful not to over stir them. When the eggs just begin to set, gently fold in the crab.

TO PREPARE LAVENDER CREAM CHEESE: Beat together all the ingredients using a mixer, or blend in a food processor, or mix together by hand until all the ingredients are well combined.

TO SERVE: Spread the toasted bagels with the lavender cream cheese and top with the crab scramble.

WINE
RECOMMENDATIONS:

DOMAINE STE. MICHELLE
*Brut Sparkling Wine,
Columbia Valley*

SNOQUALMIE
*Naked Riesling,
Columbia Valley*

Fresh Fish, Shiitake, and Vegetable Skewers

FOR MARINADE:

2 tablespoons vegetable oil

¼ cup Sauvignon Blanc

½ teaspoon sesame oil

1 tablespoon rice vinegar

1 tablespoon soy sauce

Juice of ½ lemon

Juice of ½ lime

1 to 2 tablespoons sweet chili sauce

2 cloves garlic, mashed

1 tablespoon chopped fresh cilantro

FOR SKEWERS:

1 pound peeled raw prawns

1 pound ahi tuna, cut into ½- x ½- inch squares

1 cup fresh shiitake mushrooms

1 cup cut zucchini, cut into ½- x ½- inch slices

1 cup yellow squash, cut into ½- x ½- inch slices

1 cup yellow onion, cut into ½- x ½- inch slices

1 cup red pepper, cut into ½- x ½- inch squares

TO PREPARE MARINADE: Mix all the ingredients together in a medium bowl or shake in a jar.

TO PREPARE SKEWERS: Preheat an outdoor grill on medium heat.

Thread the prawns, tuna, mushrooms, and vegetables onto skewers.

Grill the skewers on medium heat, basting often with the marinade.

My favorite foods, prepared with an Asian marinade, and cooked outside on the grill—this is an ideal summer meal.

WINE RECOMMENDATIONS:

CHATEAU STE. MICHELLE
*Sauvignon Blanc,
Columbia Valley*

COLUMBIA CREST
*Two Vines Merlot,
Columbia Valley*

ISLAND SEA BASS

Pacific halibut is a great substitute for sea bass. By cooking inside a "boat" made from aluminum foil, the fish is steamed inside and stays tender.

FOR MARINADE:

1 tablespoon lemon juice

1 tablespoon lime juice

1 tablespoon orange juice

¼ cup Riesling or Sauvignon Blanc

1 teaspoon peanut oil

1 teaspoon sesame oil

1 teaspoon chopped garlic

1 teaspoon peeled chopped fresh ginger

2 Roma tomatoes, diced

½ cup diced papaya

¼ cup diced red onion

1 tablespoon chopped fresh cilantro

1 tablespoon chopped fresh basil

Pinch salt

FOR FISH:

1 (1½-pound) sea bass fillet

FOR SERVING:

4 cups mixed field greens

TO PREPARE MARINADE: Lightly mix all the marinade ingredients in a dish large enough for fish. Place the fish into the dish and marinate 30 to 60 minutes.

TO PREPARE FISH: Preheat the grill on medium heat.

Make a large boat-shaped bowl out of aluminum foil. Place the fish in the boat and pour the marinade over the fish. Place the boat on the grill and cook with the lid closed until the fish flakes easily, about 12 to 15 minutes.

TO SERVE: Arrange the mixed greens on a serving platter. Place the fish on top of the greens. Spoon the cooked sauce from the boat over the fish.

WINE RECOMMENDATIONS:

CHATEAU STE. MICHELLE
Indian Wells Riesling, Columbia Valley

OR

Horse Heaven Vineyard Sauvignon Blanc, Horse Heaven Hills

Mahi-Mahi

FOR SAUCE:

2 tablespoons olive oil

⅛ cup Sauvignon Blanc

2 cloves garlic, mashed

2 tablespoons chopped Italian parsley

1 tablespoon chopped capers

½ teaspoon dry mustard

Juice of ½ lemon

Pinch salt

FOR FISH:

1 (2-pound) mahi-mahi fillet

TO PREPARE SAUCE: Mix the sauce ingredients together in a small bowl.

TO PREPARE FISH: Pour the sauce over the fish and let stand for 15 minutes.

Preheat the oven to 375°F.

Place the fish fillets in a baking pan. Bake in preheated oven, occasionally spooning some of the sauce over the fish while it cooks. Bake for about 15 minutes, or until the fish flakes easily.

For a mouthwatering trio, consider serving this Hawaiian fish with crispy wontons and Ahi Poke on page 88.

WINE RECOMMENDATIONS:

COLUMBIA CREST
Grand Estates Chardonnay, Columbia Valley

ERATH
Oregon Pinot Noir

SEA BASS CROATIAN-STYLE

Life and food are very simple in Croatia, especially in the small villages. The humble ingredients in this recipe reflect the simple flavors of Croatia.

FOR BASTE:

¼ cup olive oil

Juice of 1 lemon, about 3 tablespoons

¼ cup Sauvignon Blanc

2 cloves garlic, mashed

2 tablespoons chopped fresh Italian
  parsley

Pinch salt

Pinch black pepper

FOR FISH:

1 (3-pound) whole sea bass, snapper, or rockfish

TO PREPARE BASTE: Mix the ingredients together in a small bowl.

TO PREPARE FISH: Preheat an outdoor grill on medium heat.

Baste the snapper or rockfish and place on grill. Grill over medium heat, about 10 minutes per side, basting often.

WINE
RECOMMENDATIONS:

CHATEAU STE. MICHELLE
*Sauvignon Blanc,
Columbia Valley*

ERATH
Willamette Valley Pinot Blanc

Prawn and Feta Pasta with Basil

*Easy and delicious.
For the best tasting result,
seek out the freshest, most
flavorful tomatoes.*

2 pounds large prawns, cleaned

1 pound pasta (fusilli, penne, linguine)

2 tablespoons olive oil

1 yellow onion, julienned

1 small fennel bulb, julienned

3 cloves garlic, finely sliced

2 cups chopped Roma tomatoes (optional)

⅛ cup white wine

1 tablespoon lemon juice

¼ cup crumbled feta or goat cheese

¼ cup chopped fresh basil

Clean, devein, and peel the prawns; set aside.

Bring water to a boil in a stockpot. Add the pasta and cook according to package directions, until al dente. Drain.

Heat the oil over medium heat in a skillet. Sauté the onion, fennel, and garlic in the oil until the vegetables are soft. Add the tomatoes; simmer for 5 minutes. Add the wine and lemon juice and slightly reduce the heat. Add the prawns; cook until pink. Add the feta cheese; simmer until the cheese just begins to melt. Stir in the basil.

To serve, pour the prawns with the sauce over the cooked pasta.

WINE
RECOMMENDATIONS:

COLUMBIA CREST
*Grand Estates Sauvignon Blanc,
Columbia Valley*

OR

*Two Vines Vineyard 10 Rose,
Columbia Valley*

SEARED ALASKA KING SALMON WITH CHANTERELLE MUSHROOMS

With the fresh salmon and wonderful chanterelle sauce all that is needed to complete this dish is simple steamed rice.

FOR RICE:

1 cup white rice

2 cups water

FOR SALMON:

4 (4-ounce) salmon fillets

Pinch salt

Pinch pepper

1 tablespoons olive oil

1 tablespoon butter

FOR CHANTERELLE SAUCE:

2 tablespoons chopped pancetta or bacon

1 garlic clove, mashed

2 medium shallots, thinly sliced

½ pound fresh chanterelle mushrooms

⅛ cup Chardonnay

½ cup chicken broth

1 tablespoons Dijon mustard

1 tablespoons chopped fresh thyme

2 tablespoons cream

TO PREPARE RICE: Bring the rice and water to a boil in a saucepan with a lid; reduce heat, cover, and leave to cook until tender, about 15 minutes.

TO PREPARE SALMON: Season the salmon with the salt and pepper. Heat the olive oil and butter in a sauté pan to medium-high. Sear the salmon fillets on both sides, about 3 minutes per side. Remove the salmon from the pan and place on a serving platter.

TO PREPARE CHANTERELLE SAUCE: In the same sauté pan as was used for the salmon, add the pancetta and cook until crispy. Add the garlic and shallots and sauté until soft, about 4 minutes. Add the chanterelle mushrooms and sauté until soft. Stir in the wine, chicken broth, Dijon mustard, and thyme. Simmer for a few minutes until reduced. Stir the cream into the sauce. Season the sauce with salt to taste.

TO SERVE: Pour the chanterelle sauce over the salmon and serve with the steamed rice.

Seared Halibut with Clams in a Saffron-Chorizo Sauce on Grilled Polenta Cake

FOR POLENTA:

2½ cups chicken stock

1 cup polenta

2 teaspoons extra virgin olive oil

1 whole garlic bulb, roasted (see page 222) and mashed

½ cup grated Parmesan cheese

1 tablespoon butter

⅛ cup heavy cream

Pinch salt

FOR CHORIZO:

2 tablespoons olive oil

⅛ cup sliced cured chorizo

FOR SAUCE:

3 cloves garlic, mashed

1 yellow onion, julienned

3 Roma tomatoes, diced

2 or 3 sprigs thyme

1 bay leaf

Pinch saffron

⅛ cup Sauvignon Blanc

FOR FISH:

4 (4-ounce) halibut fillets (sea bass or other white fish can be substituted)

Pinch salt

Pinch pepper

2 tablespoons olive oil

FOR CLAMS:

Scant ⅛ teaspoon lemon zest

1 pound clams

FOR GARNISH:

⅓ cup chopped fresh basil

Start this dish a day ahead since the polenta will need time to firm before grilling

TO PREPARE POLENTA: In a heavy saucepan, bring the chicken stock to simmer. Add the polenta and stir constantly for 15 minutes. Add the olive oil, roasted garlic, Parmesan, butter, cream, and salt. Simmer 5 additional minutes.

Pour into a 6- by 8-inch baking dish and chill until firm. Remove the polenta from the dish and cut into wedges.

Preheat an outdoor grill on hot heat or the oven to 350°F.

Grill the polenta cake on the hot barbecue or place in preheated oven for about 10 to 15 minutes.

Seared Halibut with Clams (continued).

TO PREPARE CHORIZO: Heat the olive oil in a large high-sided sauté pan. Brown the chorizo quickly in the olive oil; remove from the pan and set aside.

TO PREPARE SAUCE: Add the garlic and onion to the same pan used to cook the chorizo. Sauté the garlic and onion until soft. Add the tomatoes, thyme, bay leaf, saffron, and wine. Reduce the heat and simmer until slightly thickened. Remove the sauce from the heat. Purée the sauce using a blender or a hand-held blender. Set sauce aside.

TO PREPARE FISH: Season the fish with salt and pepper. Heat the oil to medium-high in a sauté pan. Sauté the fish for about 3 minutes per side. Remove the fish from the pan.

TO PREPARE CLAMS: Pour the puréed sauce back into the pan used to cook the fish. Add the lemon zest, chorizo, and clams. Cover and cook until the clams open.

TO SERVE: Pour one quarter of the liquid into a flat soup bowl. Place a square of the grilled polenta on top of the sauce. Place the halibut on the polenta and surround the halibut with the clams and chorizo pieces. Garnish with the chopped fresh basil.

Sicilian-Style Halibut

1 (2-pound) halibut fillet

3 tablespoons olive oil

4 Roma tomatoes, chopped

3 cloves garlic, thinly sliced

⅛ cup Sauvignon Blanc

1 tablespoon lemon juice

1 tablespoon chopped capers

⅛ cup mixed olives (Kalamata, large green, etc.)

⅛ cup chopped fresh basil

2 tablespoons chopped fresh Italian parsley

Pinch salt

Preheat the oven to 375°F.

Place halibut in a baking dish. Mix together all sauce ingredients. Pour the sauce over the fish.

Bake in preheated oven for 10 minutes, or until the fish flakes easily with a fork.

Halibut is the perfect partner for this robust Mediterranean sauce.

WINE
RECOMMENDATIONS:

ERATH
Oregon Pinot Gris

COLUMBIA CREST
Grand Estates Shiraz, Columbia Valley

MARINATED SOCKEYE SALMON

Sockeye is one of the most flavorful of the salmon family. It is a highly sought after fresh fish, as it has a firm texture and distinctive red-orange flesh.

FOR MARINADE:

¼ cup olive oil

¼ cup Chardonnay

1 teaspoon lemon juice

½ tablespoons Dijon mustard

2 cloves garlic, mashed

¼ cup chopped fresh basil

½ teaspoon Italian Parsley

¼ teaspoon salt

¼ teaspoon white pepper

FOR FISH:

1 (3- to 4-pound) sockeye salmon

3 lemons, thinly sliced

TO PREPARE MARINADE: Mix all the marinade ingredients together.

TO PREPARE FISH: Preheat an outdoor grill on hot heat.

Make a large foil envelope and place the fish in the middle. Pour the marinade over the fish. Top the fish with the lemon slices. Seal the foil and cook on the hot grill until done, about 20 minutes.

WINE RECOMMENDATIONS:

CHATEAU STE. MICHELLE
*Cold Creek Vineyard
Chardonnay,
Columbia Valley*

OR

*Ethos Reserve Syrah,
Columbia Valley*

MARINADES

FOR VEGETABLES, PRAWNS, AND SQUID:

¼ cup extra virgin olive oil

2 tablespoons Sauvignon Blanc

Juice of 1 lemon

2 tablespoons chopped fresh parsley

2 tablespoons chopped fresh basil

Pinch red pepper flakes

1 teaspoon Dijon mustard

Pinch salt

Mix all the ingredients together thoroughly. Use as a marinade and baste.

FOR CHICKEN:

¼ cup peanut oil

½ teaspoon sesame oil

2 tablespoons soy sauce

2 tablespoons Dry Riesling

1 tablespoon rice vinegar

1 tablespoon lemon juice

2 tablespoons honey

1 tablespoon peeled chopped
 ginger

½ tablespoon chopped garlic

1 tablespoon chopped fresh cilantro

1 tablespoon dry mustard

Mix all the ingredients together thoroughly. Use as marinade and baste.

The only difficult part is deciding which foods to bathe with these delicious marinades. Prawns are a true delicacy all around the Pacific Rim. Squid is an important ingredient in many Mediterranean recipes. (Cook squid quickly, for only about four minutes, to achieve a tender succulent result.) The Asian-style marinade transforms chicken and is nice served with Jasmine rice.

WINE
RECOMMENDATIONS:

*Sauvingnon Blanc,
Washington State*

OR

*Dry Riesling,
Washington State*

Pacific Coast Oyster Stew

For a quality "company's coming" meal that will satisfy seafood lovers, all you need is this oyster stew, a good loaf of bread, and a Bibb lettuce salad. Dress the salad with a splash of lemon juice, some olive oil, and several quartered tomatoes.

2 tablespoons butter
1 onion, julienned
4 baby leeks, thinly sliced
6 fingerling or Yukon gold potatoes, quartered
1 garlic clove, mashed
½ cup chicken stock
⅛ cup Chardonnay
⅓ cup cream or half-and-half
1 teaspoon lemon juice
1 teaspoon chopped fresh tarragon
Pinch cayenne pepper
Pinch salt
12 fresh shucked oysters or 1 (1-pint) container pre-shucked oysters

Heat the butter in a sauté pan over medium heat. Sauté the onions and leeks in the butter until very soft, stirring frequently, about 10 minutes. Add the potatoes and sauté for another 5 minutes. Add the chicken stock and wine and simmer until the potatoes begin to soften. Add the cream, lemon juice, tarragon, cayenne pepper, and salt. Simmer until thickened, about 5 minutes. Add the oysters and their liquid and cook just until the oysters are plump—no more than 5 minutes.

Wine
Recommendations:

Columbia Crest
*Grand Estates Chardonnay,
Columbia Valley*

Stag's Leap Wine Cellars
*Karia Napa Valley
Chardonnay*

Prawns with Curry Mayonnaise

FOR PRAWNS:

2 pounds spot prawns or gulf prawns

2 quarts water

¼ cup Semillon

3 cloves garlic, whole

6 black peppercorns

Juice of ½ lemon

Pinch red pepper flakes

Pinch salt

FOR YOGURT-CURRY DIP:

½ cup yogurt

1 tablespoon mayonnaise

1 tablespoon lemon juice

2 cloves garlic, mashed

½ teaspoon curry powder

Fresh chopped cilantro, for garnish

TO PREPARE PRAWNS: Clean, devein, and peel the prawns; set aside.

Place all the other ingredients into a saucepan over medium-hot heat. Bring to a boil and boil for 10 minutes. Add the prawns and cook until tender and their color changes to red.

TO PREPARE YOGURT-CURRY DIP: Blend together the dip ingredients, except the cilantro. Serve in a small bowl. Garnish the dip with the cilantro.

Serve this fresh-tasting yogurt-curry combination as a dip for these easy-to-prepare prawns.

WINE
RECOMMENDATIONS:

CHATEAU STE. MICHELLE
*Cold Creek Vineyard Riesling,
Columbia Valley*

DOMAINE STE. MICHELLE
*Brut Sparkling Wine,
Columbia Valley*

ROASTED SALMON WITH WINE AND CREAM REDUCTION SAUCE

Matching rich dishes and rich wine is one way to make a perfect pairing. A Chardonnay from Washington or California will balance well with this dish.

FOR SAUCE:

2 tablespoons butter

1 tablespoon olive oil

2 large shallots, thinly sliced

2 medium size leeks, cleaned, halved lengthwise, thinly sliced

½ cup Chardonnay

¼ cup chicken stock

½ cup cream

1 tablespoon Dijon mustard

1 teaspoon lemon juice

⅛ teaspoon lemon zest

Salt, to taste

White pepper, to taste

1 teaspoon fresh tarragon leaves

FOR SALMON:

1 (2-pound) salmon fillet

1 tablespoon olive oil

1 clove garlic, mashed

Pinch salt

Pinch white pepper

½ cup Chardonnay

FOR GARNISH:

Fresh tarragon

2 lemons, sliced

TO PREPARE SAUCE: Heat the butter and olive oil in a large, high-sided sauté pan, over medium heat. Sauté the shallots and leeks for 5 minutes. Add the wine and chicken stock. Reduce heat to simmer. Cover and cook until the leeks are soft. Uncover and add the cream, Dijon mustard, lemon juice, and zest. Season with salt and white pepper, to taste. Continue to simmer until reduced by half. Add tarragon leaves.

TO PREPARE SALMON: Preheat the oven to 425°F. Place the salmon in a baking pan. Mix the olive oil, garlic, salt, and white pepper together. Brush the olive oil mixture over the salmon. Pour ½ cup of the wine around the salmon. Bake for about 12 minutes or until fish flakes easily.

TO SERVE: Spoon the sauce onto a platter and place the salmon on top. Garnish with the fresh tarragon leaves and lemon slices.

WINE RECOMMENDATIONS:

CHATEAU STE. MICHELLE
Ethos Reserve Chardonnay, Columbia Valley

ANTICA NAPA VALLEY
Chardonnay

SEAFOOD SAGANAKI

1 cup rice or ziti pasta

¼ cup olive oil

1 onion, chopped

3 cloves garlic, chopped

1 (14-ounce) can crushed tomatoes in
 purée

¼ cup white wine

Juice of ½ lemon

Pinch red pepper flakes

1 pound prawns, peeled and deveined

⅓ pound calamari

4 ounces feta cheese

⅓ cup chopped fresh basil, for garnish

Cook the rice or pasta according to package directions.

Heat the olive oil in a large skillet over medium high heat. Sauté the onion
and garlic in oil until soft. Stir in the tomatoes, wine, and lemon juice. Add the
pepper flakes, to taste. Simmer for 7 to 10 minutes. Add the seafood; continue to
simmer until the prawns change color, about 5 minutes. Crumble the feta cheese
into the seafood; continue to cook until the cheese melts, about 3 minutes.

Serve the seafood and sauce over the rice or pasta. Garnish with the
chopped basil.

*Greek in origin, Saganaki
takes its name from the
two-handled pan in
which it is cooked. Serve
it as it would be served
in Greece—accompanied
by a glass of wine, fresh
tomatoes, olives, and
bread. You might even
want to shout, "Opa!"*

WINE
RECOMMENDATIONS:

CHATEAU STE. MICHELLE
*Horse Heaven Vineyard
Sauvignon Blanc,
Horse Heaven Hills*

OR

*Pinot Gris,
Columbia Valley*

SEAFOOD RISOTTO

This recipe serves four as a main or six to eight as a side dish. Sometimes, at the last minute, I will stir in frozen peas that have been thawed, not cooked.

The hot rice will cook them somewhat, and they retain their bright green coloring. For a simple and complete meal, serve this with a light oil and vinegar salad.

FOR RISOTTO:

2 tablespoons olive oil
2 tablespoons butter
1 large onion, finely chopped
1 large head of fennel, finely chopped
⅛ cup chopped celery leaves
3 cloves garlic, minced
2 to 3 Roma tomatoes, finely chopped
Pinch cayenne pepper

Pinch saffron threads
⅛ cup Sauvignon Blanc
Pinch salt
2 cups Arborio rice
1 quart (4 cups) chicken stock
1 tablespoon butter
⅓ cup cream

FOR SEAFOOD:

1 tablespoon olive oil
1 tablespoon butter
1 clove garlic, chopped
⅓ pound mussels, cleaned
⅓ pound clams, cleaned

⅓ pound scallops, cleaned
⅓ pound prawns, cleaned
⅛ cup Sauvignon Blanc
Juice of ½ lemon

FOR BASIL-ONION-GARLIC:

½ cup basil leaves
3 green onions
1 garlic clove

2 tablespoons olive oil
⅛ teaspoon orange zest

FOR GARNISH:

¼ cup Parmesan cheese

Chopped fresh Italian parsley

WINE
RECOMMENDATIONS:

COLUMBIA CREST
*Two Vines Sauvignon Blanc,
Columbia Valley*

ERATH
Oregon Pinot Gris

TO PREPARE RISOTTO: Heat the oil and butter in a large high-sided pot (6- to 8-quart) over medium heat. Sauté the onion, fennel, celery leaves, and garlic until very wilted, about 20 minutes. Add the tomatoes and simmer until completely mixed into the sauce. This should not look like tomato sauce but just have a whisper of tomato. Add the cayenne pepper, saffron, wine, and salt. Simmer another 5 minutes. Add the rice and stir until the rice has absorbed the sauce. Add 1 cup of the chicken stock and stir until absorbed. Continue the process until the rice is tender (al dente).

TO PREPARE SEAFOOD: Heat the olive oil and butter in a sauté pan over high heat. Sauté the garlic and all the seafood for 2 minutes over high heat. Add a splash of wine and the juice of a half lemon. Simmer 2 more minutes. Remove from heat.

TO COMPLETE RISOTTO: When the risotto is almost al dente, stir in the butter and cream. Place the seafood in the risotto; cover and simmer until shells are open, about 5 to 7 minutes.

TO PREPARE BASIL-ONION-GARLIC: Very finely chop these ingredients together. Place in a small bowl and moisten with a small amount of olive oil. Add scant amount of orange zest if desired. Set aside.

TO SERVE: Spoon the seafood risotto into bowls and garnish with the reserved basil-onion-garlic mixture, grated Parmesan cheese, and chopped Italian parsley.

SEARED WILD KING SALMON AND VEGETABLES IN ASIAN BROTH

EXECUTIVE CHEF JANET HEDSTROM, CHATEAU STE. MICHELLE WINERY

Adding some cooked rice to each bowl is a great addition to make a meal.

FOR GINGER REDUCTION:

¾ cup lemon juice

¼ cup lime juice

1 cup sugar

¾ cup grated fresh ginger

¼ cup pickled ginger

FOR ASIAN BROTH:

1½ cup dry white wine

¾ cup soy sauce

¾ cup Ginger Reduction (recipe above)

1 teaspoon hot chili sesame oil

2¼ teaspoon fish sauce

3 teaspoon lime juice

1 teaspoon kosher salt

FOR SALMON:

6 (4-ounce) salmon fillets, skin removed

Asian Broth (recipe above)

Olive oil

1 large carrot, peeled and thinly julienned

1 (2-inch) piece of ginger, peeled and cut into thick julienne pieces

FOR VEGETABLES:

6 green onions, thinly sliced at an angle

¾ cup asparagus, thinly sliced at an angle

1 cup finely shredded red cabbage

¼ cup basil, torn into medium sized pieces

¼ cup cilantro leaves pulled from the stem

1 tablespoon mint leaves, coarsely chopped

Basil oil, to taste (optional)

Sesame oil, to taste (optional)

TO PREPARE GINGER REDUCTION: Place all the ingredients in a small saucepan and bring to a boil over medium high heat. Simmer for 2 to 3 minutes, then remove from the heat and let cool to room temperature. Strain and reserve the liquid.

TO PREPARE ASIAN BROTH: Combine all the ingredients and whisk together thoroughly. Measure about 2½ cups of the liquid and set aside for baking the salmon. The remaining amount will be used as a marinade.

TO PREPARE SALMON: Place the salmon in a bowl, and pour the remaining Asian Broth over the salmon. Toss to coat, then marinate for at least 5 minutes, but no more than 10 minutes.

Remove the fish from the marinade and pat dry. Heat a medium sauté pan over medium-high heat. Add enough olive oil to barely coat the bottom of the pan; then add the salmon and brown on both sides.

Preheat the oven to 400°F.

Bring the reserved 2½ cups of broth to a boil. Place the julienned carrots and ginger in a shallow baking dish, top with the salmon pieces. Pour the heated broth over the fish and cover with foil. Place in the oven and cook until the fish is barely done, about 4 to 6 minutes, depending on thickness.

TO PREPARE VEGETABLES: While the fish is cooking, heat six serving bowls. When warmed, divide the asparagus, red cabbage, green onion, and herbs between the bowls. Remove the fish from the oven and place a piece of fish in each bowl with some of the liquid. Drizzle with basil oil and a couple drops of sesame oil if desired. Serve immediately.

SICILIAN SEAFOOD PASTA

A good homemade marinara sauce can be made ahead and stored in the refrigerator to be used for another recipe such as pizza.

FOR SEAFOOD PASTA:

1 pound linguine pasta

1 teaspoon salt

¼ cup olive oil

1 onion, thinly chopped

1 fennel bulb, thinly chopped

1 red pepper, thinly chopped

3 cloves garlic, thinly sliced

¼ cup red wine vinegar

1 pound mussels, cleaned and de-bearded

½ pound clams

8 large shrimp, peeled and deveined

½ pound white fish (halibut), cut into chunks

1 cup Sicilian Marinara Sauce (see page 223)

FOR GARNISH:

¼ cup chopped fresh basil

¼ cup chopped arugula

TO PREPARE SEAFOOD PASTA: Bring water to a boil in a stockpot. Add salt. Place the linguine into the pot, stir; return to a boil, and cook pasta al dente, about 11 minutes. Drain the pasta.

Heat the olive oil in a large pan over medium heat. Sauté the onion, fennel, red pepper, and garlic until tender. Add the vinegar and bring to a boil. Stir in the mussels, clams, shrimp, and fish. Simmer until the shells just open. Add the marinara sauce and heat through.

TO SERVE: Spoon the sauce and seafood over the hot linguine noodles. Garnish with the basil and arugula.

WINE
RECOMMENDATIONS:

COL SOLARE
Red Wine,
Columbia Valley

STELLA MARIS
Red Wine,
Columbia Valley

Sweet and Sour Marlin with Coconut-Curry Rice

FOR SWEET AND SOUR FISH:

4 (5-ounce) marlin fillets

⅓ cup soy

⅓ cup chicken stock

¼ cup Riesling

1 tablespoon rice vinegar

1 teaspoon honey

1 teaspoon peanut oil

1 teaspoon sesame oil

1 tablespoon orange marmalade

2 cloves garlic, chopped

½ teaspoon peeled grated fresh ginger

1 tablespoon chopped fresh cilantro

Juice of 1 lime

Pinch pepper flakes

FOR COCONUT-CURRY RICE:

1 cup uncooked rice

1 tablespoon peanut oil

1 teaspoon chili oil

1 large onion, thinly julienned

1 small fennel bulb, thinly sliced

1 clove garlic, mashed

½ teaspoon grated ginger

2 tablespoons flour

1 cup chicken stock

¼ cup coconut milk

1 teaspoon green curry powder

FOR GARNISH:

Grapes, sliced lengthwise

Papaya or mango, cubed

TO PREPARE SWEET AND SOUR FISH: Heat all the sweet and sour ingredients, except fish, in a saucepan over medium heat. Simmer until reduced by at least half. Cool.

Preheat an outdoor grill on hot heat.

Generously baste the fish with the sweet and sour sauce. Grill the fish on the hot grill, basting often, 5 minutes per side.

TO PREPARE COCONUT-CURRY RICE: Bring the rice and 2 cups water to a boil in a saucepan. Reduce the heat; cover, and simmer for 15 minutes, until tender.

Heat the peanut and chili oils over medium heat in a saucepan. Sauté the onion, fennel, garlic, and ginger in the oils over medium heat until very soft. Sprinkle with the flour and continue stirring until the flour has well coated the vegetables. Add the chicken stock and stir until smooth. Stir in the coconut milk and curry powder. Simmer until thickened. Place the rice on a serving platter and pour the coconut-curry sauce over the rice.

TO SERVE: Place the sweet and sour fish on top of the coconut-curry rice. Garnish with a combination of sliced grapes and diced papaya and mango.

You may substitute ahi tuna or mahi-mahi for the marlin in this sweet and sour fish recipe. Use your favorite rice, such as jasmine, for this dish.

WINE RECOMMENDATIONS:

SNOQUALMIE
*Naked Riesling,
Columbia Valley*

COLUMBIA CREST
*Two Vines Merlot,
Columbia Valley*

Thai Mussels

A delicious broth like this requires plenty of crusty bread!

FOR BROTH:

1 cup coconut milk

¾ tablespoon red curry paste

Juice of ½ lime

½ teaspoon Thai fish sauce

½ cup sake

1 teaspoon minced garlic

1 teaspoon minced ginger

1 tablespoon chopped basil

FOR MUSSELS:

1 pound mussels, cleaned and bearded

TO PREPARE BROTH: Mix all the ingredients for the broth together in a saucepan with a wire whisk. Heat to boiling; reduce and simmer.

TO PREPARE MUSSELS: Place the mussels in a heavy saucepan and add enough of the broth to cover the bottom of the pan. Cover and steam until the mussels open.

TO SERVE: Transfer the mussels to individual bowls; ladle the hot broth into the bowls.

WINE
RECOMMENDATIONS:

CHATEAU STE. MICHELLE
*Gewürztraminer,
Columbia Valley*

COLUMBIA CREST
*H3 Merlot,
Horse Heaven Hills*

∞ POULTRY ∞

Smoked Duck and Asian Slaw Salad with Ginger-Plum Chutney

Uncooked chutney is great for summertime dining. The fruit has more acidity and tastes lighter. For winter fare, cooked chutney has a deeper flavor and will keep in the refrigerator for a few days.

FOR GINGER-PLUM CHUTNEY:

1 cup diced fresh plums

1 tablespoon peanut oil (optional)

1 small red onion, diced

⅛ teaspoon grated fresh ginger

1 tablespoon rice vinegar

Pinch cayenne pepper

Pinch salt

FOR DUCK AND ASIAN SLAW SALAD:

2 tablespoons peanut oil, divided

½ teaspoon sesame oil

2 cloves garlic, sliced

1 teaspoon peeled, grated fresh ginger

1 cup julienned Napa cabbage

3 carrots, julienned

½ cup julienned snow peas

1 cup julienned jicama

1 cup julienned shiitake mushrooms

1 tablespoon rice vinegar

1 tablespoon soy sauce

1 head Bibb (butter) lettuce, leaves arranged into "cups"

1½ cups julienned smoked duck breast

Chopped fresh cilantro, for garnish

TO PREPARE CHUTNEY: For the uncooked method toss all ingredients together and let stand for at least 1 hour before serving, but preferably overnight.

For the cooked method, heat oil in a saucepan and briefly sauté onion and ginger in oil. Add remaining ingredients and stir. When plums are just heated through, remove from heat. Serve immediately, or cool and store for future use.

TO PREPARE DUCK AND ASIAN SLAW: Heat 1 tablespoon of peanut oil, sesame oil, garlic, and ginger in a large saucepan. Add cabbage, carrots, peas, jicama, and mushrooms. Sauté over high heat until just wilted, about 2 minutes. Remove from heat and toss with rice vinegar, remainder of the peanut oil, and soy sauce. Place in lettuce cups and top with smoked duck breast. Garnish with cilantro.

WINE RECOMMENDATIONS:

COLUMBIA CREST
Grand Estates Merlot,
Columbia Valley

CHATEAU STE. MICHELLE
Syrah,
Columbia Valley

GRILLED QUAIL WITH POBLANO CORNBREAD PUDDING AND MOLE

CHEF SCOTT HARBERTS, CHATEAU STE. MICHELLE WINERY

FOR QUAIL:

6 quail	Pinch salt
1 tablespoon olive oil	Pinch black pepper

FOR MOLE:

1 cup chopped onion	½ cup Syrah
4 cloves garlic	3 cup chicken stock
3 dried California chiles	1 cup beef stock
1 cup chopped red bell pepper	1 teaspoon dried oregano
1 cinnamon stick	½ cup currants
1 tablespoon star anise	½ cup raisins
10 cloves	½ cup toasted almonds
2 teaspoon cumin	¼ cup toasted pine nuts
2 tablespoon chili powder	½ cup Mexican chocolate

FOR CORNBREAD:

1 cup diced onion	1 teaspoon chili powder
4 cloves garlic, chopped	½ teaspoon dried oregano
1 cup cornmeal	¾ cup milk
1 cup flour	2 eggs
¼ cup sugar	1 (14-ounce) can creamed corn
1 teaspoon salt	½ cup roasted and diced poblano
1 tablespoon baking powder	peppers
1 teaspoon cumin	1 cup grated Cheddar cheese

TO PREPARE QUAIL: Preheat an outdoor grill on medium heat.

Rub the quail with the olive oil and season with salt and pepper.

Cook on preheated grill for 5 minutes per side, or until the quail reaches your desired doneness.

TO PREPARE MOLE: Sauté the onions, garlic, chiles, and pepper. Cook until the onion and garlic are slightly browned, about 10 minutes. Add the cinnamon, anise, clove, cumin, and chili powder. Cook 1 more minute. Deglaze the pan with the wine, and reduce to ¼ cup. Add the two stocks and bring to a boil.

The bold flavor of quail can hold up to the bold flavors of this zesty Mexican-influenced platter. It's downright delicious.

WINE RECOMMENDATIONS:

CHATEAU STE. MICHELLE
Ethos Reserve Syrah, Columbia Valley

ERATH
Oregon Pinot Noir

Grilled Quail with Poblano Cornbread Pudding and Mole (continued).

Reduce heat and simmer for 20 minutes. Add the currants, raisins, almonds, and pine nuts. Cook for 15 more minutes. Turn off the heat and add the chocolate. Stir to melt, then purée the sauce. Pass through a strainer and serve.

TO PREPARE CORNBREAD: Preheat an oven to 350°F.

Over medium heat, sauté the onion and garlic until carmelized, about 10 minutes; Cool. Combine all the dry ingredients together in a bowl. Whisk together the milk and eggs. Pour the wet ingredients into the dry ingredients and mix well. Add the creamed corn, peppers, and cheese. Mix well. Pour into a prepared 8-inch by 10-inch baking dish. Bake for 40 minutes, or until a toothpick comes out clean.

Herb Roasted Chicken with Penne Pasta

2 tablespoons olive oil

2 tablespoons chopped fresh Italian parsley

2 tablespoons chopped fresh rosemary

⅛ cup Pinot Gris

2 tablespoons lemon juice

1 teaspoon dry mustard

¼ teaspoon salt

1 fryer chicken, cut into 8 pieces

3 tablespoons olive oil

2 large yellow onions, cut large julienne

5 cloves garlic, halved

4 Roma tomatoes, cut into large pieces

½ cup coarsely chopped fresh basil

½ cup Pinot Gris or other dry white wine

¼ cup chicken stock

½ teaspoon salt

1 pound penne pasta

Parmesan cheese, for garnish

Chopped fresh basil, for garnish

Mix the olive oil, parsley, rosemary, wine, lemon juice, mustard, and salt together in a large flat dish. Toss the chicken together with the marinade until the chicken is completely coated. Allow the chicken to marinate at least 1 hour.

Preheat the oven to 350°F.

Heat the olive oil in a large ovenproof skillet or Dutch oven over medium heat. Sauté the onions and garlic until wilted. Remove from the heat. Add the tomatoes, basil, wine, chicken stock, and salt.

Lay the marinated chicken skin-side-up on top of the onion mixture. Bake in the oven for 45 minutes, or until the chicken is nicely browned.

Bring water to a boil in a 6-quart pot. Add penne pasta and cook until al dente, about 10 to 12 minutes. Drain.

Remove the chicken from the oven and transfer chicken to a serving platter; cover with foil to keep warm.

To serve, place the pan with the onion mixture over medium heat. Reduce the juices until slightly thickened. Toss the sauce with the penne pasta.

Transfer the pasta to a serving platter. Arrange the cooked chicken on the pasta. Garnish with the Parmesan cheese and chopped basil.

Chicken that is embedded with herbs and seasonings, cooked with a flavorful broth until it practically falls off the bone—what's not to love.

HONEY-MERLOT QUAIL

The main tips you need to know for preparing quail are that it's good to marinate it for a long period of time (overnight is best), and to cook it for a short period of time (10 minutes is all). Following these two pointers will produce flavorful, tender meat.

A sweet and savory marinade complements the pleasantly gamey quail. You can substitute chicken breasts, just be sure to thoroughly cook them.

WINE
RECOMMENDATIONS:

NORTH STAR
Merlot,
Columbia Valley

SPRING VALLEY VINEYARD
Nine Lee Syrah,
Walla Walla Valley

FOR MARINADE:

¼ cup Merlot

¼ cup balsamic vinegar

2 tablespoons olive oil

1 teaspoon Dijon mustard

1 tablespoon honey

2 cloves garlic, mashed

1 teaspoon chopped fresh Italian parsley

1 teaspoon chopped fresh rosemary

1 teaspoon chopped fresh thyme

⅛ teaspoon salt

⅛ teaspoon black pepper

FOR QUAIL:

4 whole quail

TO PREPARE MARINADE: Mix all the marinade ingredients together in a small bowl.

TO PREPARE QUAIL: Place the quail in a baking dish. Pour the marinade over the quail and leave to marinate overnight if possible, or at least 1 hour.

Preheat an outdoor grill on medium heat.

Grill the quail over medium heat, 5 minutes per side.

MUSHROOM-STUFFED GAME HENS WITH SOY-MERLOT SAUCE

FOR SOY-MERLOT SAUCE:

½ cup soy sauce

½ cup Merlot

1 tablespoon olive oil

2 cloves garlic, mashed

1 tablespoon orange marmalade

Pinch of lemon or orange zest

1 teaspoon thyme

1 teaspoon dry mustard

FOR MUSHROOM STUFFING:

1 tablespoon olive oil

1 tablespoon butter

1 red bell pepper, diced

1 yellow bell pepper, diced

1 yellow onion, diced

1 clove garlic, mashed

½- ¾-pound chanterelle mushrooms

Splash of Sauvignon Blanc

1 teaspoon chopped fresh Italian parsley

1 teaspoon chopped fresh sage

1 teaspoon chopped fresh rosemary

1 teaspoon chopped fresh thyme

½ teaspoon salt

½ teaspoon black pepper

2 cups small bread cubes

1 cup chicken stock

FOR GAME HENS:

4 whole game hens (or 4 half chicken breasts)

4 slices prosciutto or pancetta

TO PREPARE SAUCE: Mix all the ingredients together in a saucepan. Simmer until reduced by half, about 20 minutes.

TO PREPARE STUFFING: Heat the olive oil and butter in a saucepan or sauté pan. Sauté the red pepper, yellow pepper, onion, garlic, and mushrooms until they are just soft. Add the wine. Remove the pan from the heat. Stir the parsley, sage, rosemary, thyme, salt, and pepper into the mixture. Let cool.

Moisten the bread cubes with chicken stock. Stir the bread cubes into the sautéed vegetables.

TO PREPARE GAME HENS: Preheat an outdoor grill to hot, or preheat the oven to 350°F.

Make a slit in the breast of each game hen and stuff with the mushroom stuffing. Wrap each game hen with the prosciutto or pancetta.

To cook on the grill, preheat grill to medium-hot.

Baste the game hens with sauce and place on the grill. Cook, basting frequently, about 5 minutes per side.

To cook in the oven, preheat oven to 350°F. Bake for 25 minutes.

Game hens are kept quite moist by stuffing the boned breast cavities and wrapping them in prosciutto. As long as they aren't over cooked they will be tender and juicy. Chicken breast is a good substitute for the game hens, just be sure to cook them thoroughly.

WINE RECOMMENDATIONS:

CHATEAU STE. MICHELLE
*Canoe Ridge Estate Merlot,
Horse Heaven Hills*

COLUMBIA CREST
*Walter Clore
Private Reserve Red,
Columbia Valley*

Oven "Fried" Chicken

½ cup olive oil

2 cloves garlic, mashed

1 large fryer chicken, cut into pieces

Salt

Black pepper

2 cups unseasoned fine bread crumbs

2 tablespoons chopped fresh rosemary

2 tablespoons chopped fresh Italian parsley

2 tablespoon chopped fresh oregano

¼ cup grated Parmesan cheese

Mix the garlic and olive oil in a shallow dish or bowl and let stand about 1 hour.

Preheat the oven to 325°F.

Season the chicken pieces with salt and pepper and roll in olive oil until well coated. Mix together the bread crumbs, rosemary, parsley, oregano, and Parmesan cheese. Roll the chicken pieces in the seasoned bread crumbs and place on a baking pan.

Roast in the preheated oven for about 20 minutes. Turn the chicken and roast for another 20 minutes. The chicken is cooked when the juices run clear when poked with a fork.

Wine Recommendations:

Snoqualmie
*Naked Riesling,
Columbia Valley*

Chateau Ste. Michelle
*Chardonnay,
Columbia Valley*

Pastitsada

½ cup olive oil

1 whole fryer chicken, cut into 8 pieces

4 large onions, thinly julienned

6 whole cloves garlic

½ cup Sauvignon Blanc

½ cup chicken stock

1 (6-ounce) can tomato paste

1 cup chopped Roma tomatoes

2 sticks cinnamon

⅛ teaspoon ground cloves

⅛ teaspoon grated nutmeg

Salt, to taste

Black pepper, to taste

1 pound macaroni

Grated Parmesan cheese, for garnish

Chopped fresh oregano, for garnish

Heat the oil in a large high-sided sauté pan with a lid. Brown the chicken on all sides. Once the chicken is browned, remove from the pan. Add the onion and garlic. Sauté over medium heat until onion softens. Add the tomatoes and continue to cook for another 5 minutes. Mix together the chicken stock, wine, and tomato paste; pour into the onion mixture. Add the cinnamon sticks, cloves, and nutmeg. Season with salt and pepper to taste. Mix thoroughly. Return the chicken to the pan; cover.

Heat the oven to 325°F and bake for 1 hour. Alternatively, simmer on the stove, over low heat, for 1 hour.

While the chicken is cooking, bring water to a boil in a large saucepan, add macaroni and cook al dente, about 9 minutes.

To serve, remove the chicken from the sauce; keep the chicken warm. Remove the cinnamon sticks. Mix the sauce with the cooked and drained macaroni.

Garnish with the grated Parmesan cheese and chopped fresh oregano.

Enjoy the wonderful aroma of this dish as it cooks! This is comfort food that is served for every big occasion in Mediterranean countries such as Croatia and Greece. Cooks have their own recipes that may include chicken or beef, but it's the cinnamon and cloves that define the flavor of pastitsada.

WINE
RECOMMENDATIONS:

COLUMBIA CREST
*Grand Estates
Cabernet Sauvignon,
Columbia Valley*

OR

*Reserve Syrah,
Columbia Valley*

ROASTED ROSEMARY CHICKEN

Rosemary gives a distinctive taste and there's no skimping on the flavor in this recipe. You may prefer a little less garlic or herbs, and feel free to adjust the red pepper flakes to please your palate.

⅛ cup olive oil

¼ stick (⅛ cup) butter

4 cloves garlic, finely chopped

Juice of 1 lemon

⅛ cup Sauvignon Blanc

1 teaspoon dry mustard

2 tablespoons chopped fresh rosemary

2 tablespoons chopped Italian parsley

½ teaspoon paprika

Pinch red pepper flakes

Pinch salt

Pinch black pepper

1 large whole broiler-fryer chicken

Heat the olive oil and butter in a saucepan. Add the garlic, lemon juice, wine, mustard, rosemary, parsley, paprika, red pepper flakes, salt, and pepper. Let simmer for 5 to 7 minutes. Remove from heat.

Preheat the oven to 325°F.

Cut the chicken into 8 pieces. Baste the chicken with the sauce and cook in the oven, for 1½ hours, basting with the sauce frequently and liberally.

WINE
RECOMMENDATIONS:

SNOQUALMIE
*Naked Chardonnay,
Columbia Valley*
OR
*Syrah,
Columbia Valley*

Seared Five-Spice Duck Breast with Orange Sauce

FOR DUCK:

12 (6-ounce) marinated duck breasts

1 ounce five-spice powder

1 ounce ginger powder

Salt, to taste

Black pepper, to taste

FOR ORANGE SAUCE:

2 tablespoons butter

⅓ cup sugar

1 bottle red wine

¼ cup orange juice concentrate

2 cups demi-glace

2 juniper berries

2 whole cloves

½ cup duck sauce

Zest of 2 oranges (reserve some for garnish) (blanched)

3 ounces (¾ stick) cold butter, cut into small cubes

Salt, to taste

Black pepper, to taste

FOR MIREPOIX:

2 tablespoons butter

2 onions, diced

2 carrots, diced

2 stalks celery, diced

2 cloves garlic, mashed

2 teaspoons chopped fresh herbs (such as basil, cilantro, tarragon, thyme)

Your kitchen will smell wonderful while the duck is roasting in the oven.

TO PREPARE DUCK: Marinate the duck breast with the ginger and five-spice powder. Season with salt and pepper.

TO PREPARE ORANGE SAUCE: Heat butter in skillet, add the sugar and caramelize. Pour in the red wine and the orange juice and let reduce. When sugar is dissolved, add the demi-glace and let simmer with the juniper berries and the cloves. Add the duck sauce and the orange zest for taste and firmness. Remove the cloves and the juniper berries and whisk in the cold butter just before serving. Season with salt and pepper if needed.

TO PREPARE MIREPOIX: Heat butter in sauté pan. Add onions, carrots, celery, garlic, and herbs. Sauté until soft, about 10 minutes.

TO COMPLETE DUCK: Preheat oven to 350°F.

Pan sear duck breasts well on each side and place in hotel pan with about 1½ cups mirepoix.

Place in preheated oven and roast for 10 minutes.

TO SERVE: Pour the orange sauce on the plate first and arrange duck on top. Garnish with more orange zest.

WINE RECOMMENDATIONS:

Northstar
Walla Walla Valley Merlot

Conn Creek
Cabernet Sauvignon, Napa Valley

Sausage-Stuffed Fresh Roast Turkey

This economical feast will become a family favorite. Serve with Whole-Berry Cranberry Twist on page 224.

FOR SAUSAGE STUFFING:

2 tablespoons olive oil

2 tablespoons butter

1 large onion, chopped

2 cloves garlic, chopped

1 pound mild Italian sausage

¼ cup celery tops, chopped

1 Granny Smith apple, peeled, cored, and cubed

1 (10-ounce) package frozen chopped spinach, thawed and drained

1 teaspoon chopped fresh rosemary

1 teaspoon chopped fresh thyme

1 tablespoon chopped fresh sage

1 tablespoon chopped fresh Italian parsley

2 cups cubed dry bread

2 cups chicken stock

2 tablespoons Sauvignon Blanc

FOR TURKEY BASTE:

2 tablespoons olive oil

Juice of 2 lemons

4 cloves garlic

¼ cup Riesling

1 teaspoon chopped fresh Italian parsley

1 teaspoon chopped fresh sage

1 teaspoon chopped fresh rosemary

1 teaspoon chopped fresh thyme

Pinch black pepper

Salt, to taste

FOR TURKEY:

12 pound fresh boneless turkey

WINE RECOMMENDATIONS:

CHATEAU STE. MICHELLE
*Riesling,
Columbia Valley*

COLUMBIA CREST
*Grand Estates Shiraz,
Columbia Valley*

OR

*Gewürztraminer,
Columbia Valley*

TO PREPARE STUFFING: Heat the olive oil and butter in a large heavy skillet over medium heat. Add the onion and garlic and sauté until soft. Add the sausage; break up and cook until just done. Remove from heat and cool. Add the celery, apple, spinach, rosemary, thyme, sage, parsley, and bread cubes. Mix thoroughly. Stir in the chicken stock and wine. Stuffing should be moist but not mushy.

TO PREPARE BASTE: Blend all the basting ingredients together in a blender or food processor. Season with salt to taste.

TO PREPARE TURKEY: Preheat the oven to 400°F.

Rinse the turkey, inside and out under cold water; dry. Just before roasting, stuff the cavities; do not pack too tightly. Close the cavities using metal skewers, or sew up with cooking twine. Tie the legs together. Place the turkey on a rack in a roasting pan, immediately put into the oven and reduce the oven temperature to 300°F. Bake the turkey for 4½ hours, basting frequently.

∽ Vegetarian ∾

Arugula Frittata

2 eggs

1 cup finely chopped arugula

½ cup grated Parmesan cheese

Pinch red pepper flakes

Pinch salt

1 tablespoon butter

1 tablespoon olive oil

Lemon wedges, for serving

Scramble eggs in a medium bowl. Add arugula, Parmesan cheese, pepper flakes, and salt. Stir until well mixed.

Heat butter and olive oil in a sauté pan over medium-high heat. Place about ¼ cup of the egg mixture in the pan for each frittata. Fry until golden on both sides. Remove and place on paper towel; then transfer to a warm plate. Serve with a wedge of lemon.

All over the Mediterranean region, eggs play a vital culinary role. These mini frittatas, or fritters as they could be called, make a wonderful light lunch or simple supper when paired with a salad.

WINE
RECOMMENDATIONS:

Domaine Ste. Michelle
*Brut Sparkling Wine,
Columbia Valley*

Snoqaulmie
*Naked Chardonnay,
Columbia Valley*

CAPONATA

1 eggplant, cut into ½-inch cubes

Salt

2 tablespoons olive oil

1 large yellow onion, diced

1 red bell pepper, diced

1 yellow bell pepper, diced

2 cloves garlic, finely chopped

1 tablespoon tomato paste, mixed with
 1 tablespoon water

¼ cup chopped pitted Kalamata olives

1 tablespoon capers

2 to 4 anchovy fillets, finely chopped
 (optional)

½ teaspoon dry mustard

⅛ teaspoon ground cumin

1 tablespoon finely chopped fresh
 oregano

1 tablespoon finely chopped fresh basil

1 tablespoon finely chopped fresh Italian parsley

1 tablespoon extra virgin olive oil

1 tablespoon balsamic vinegar

1 (5-ounce) can finest albacore tuna,
 drained (optional)

 ½ teaspoon salt

Sprinkle eggplant with salt and let drain for about 20 minutes. This will back out the bitter juices. Rinse away the salt and pat dry with paper towel.

In a saucepan, heat olive oil. Sauté onion, red pepper, yellow bell pepper, and garlic until soft. Add eggplant and sauté until soft. Add tomato paste mixed with water. Season with salt. Reduce heat. Stir in remaining ingredients and heat through.

Caponata can be served as a main dish or on crostini as an appetizer. Though excellent as a vegetarian main dish, non-vegetarians may choose to make this recipe in a more traditional style and include anchovies and tuna.

WINE
RECOMMENDATIONS:

DOMAINE STE. MICHELLE
*Blanc de Noirs Sparkling Wine,
Columbia Valley*

SNOQUALMIE
*Naked Merlot,
Columbia Valley*

Chanterelle Pasta

Just imagine the texture of fleshy wild mushrooms in a creamy mascarpone and Chardonnay sauce. Pleasantly aromatic, golden chanterelles have a magical appeal.

FOR PASTA:

Pappardelle, tagliatelle, or fettuccine

FOR SAUCE:

1 tablespoon butter	⅛ cup Chardonnay
1 tablespoon olive oil	1 cup thick stock
1 medium onion, thinly julienned	¼ teaspoon fresh thyme
2 shallots, thinly sliced	1 teaspoon Dijon mustard
1 to 2 cloves garlic, mashed	2 tablespoons mascarpone
¾ pound Chanterelle mushrooms, pulled into medium pieces	Salt, to taste
	Black pepper, to taste

FOR GARNISH:

Chopped fresh Italian parsley   Freshly grated Parmesan cheese

TO PREPARE PASTA: Bring water to a boil in a large stockpot over high heat. Add pasta to the boiling water and cook according to package directions, about 8 to 10 minutes. Drain.

TO PREPARE SAUCE: While pasta is cooking, heat butter and olive oil over medium heat in a large sauté pan. Add onion, shallots, and garlic and sauté until very soft. Turn up the heat a little. Add the mushrooms and sauté until they begin to wilt, about 3 minutes. Stir in wine, stock, thyme, and Dijon mustard. Simmer until the sauce is reduced by a third. Stir in mascarpone. Season with salt and pepper to taste. Do not boil the sauce after adding the cheese as it could curdle.

TO SERVE: Serve the sauce over the hot cooked pappardelle.
    Garnish with parsley and Parmesan cheese.

WINE
RECOMMENDATIONS:

Columbia Crest
*Grand Estates Chardonnay,
Columbia Valley*

Antica Napa Valley
Chardonnay

Eggplant and Zucchini Strata

1 tablespoon butter

1 eggplant, sliced into ¼-inch rounds

2 large zucchini, sliced into ¼-inch rounds

2 to 3 tomatoes, sliced into ¼-inch rounds

1 yellow or sweet onion, thinly sliced

3 cloves garlic, finely chopped

4 whole balls fresh milk mozzarella, thinly sliced

¼ cup extra virgin olive oil

1 cup fresh basil leaves

Freshly ground black pepper

Salt, to taste

1½ cups Sicilian Marinara Sauce (see recipe on page 223) or diced canned tomatoes

⅛ cup Sauvignon Blanc

Preheat oven to 350°F.

Rub the bottom and sides of a 3- to 4-inch deep baking dish with the butter.

Make a layer of eggplant, zucchini, tomatoes, and onion. Sprinkle with garlic. Layer with mozzarella and a drizzle of olive oil. Layer with basil leaves. Sprinkle with freshly ground pepper and salt. Repeat the process for 3 layers. Pour marinara sauce or diced tomatoes around the vegetables. Sprinkle with the wine.

Cover and bake in preheated oven for 15 minutes. Uncover and bake an additional 20 minutes or until bubbling.

Who would have guessed that culinary paradise could be reached with a simple eggplant, two zucchini squash, and a few tomatoes and onions. Must be the copious amounts of basil, a good wine, and the fresh mozzarella that catapult the dish to such heights.

WINE
RECOMMENDATIONS:

Chateau Ste. Michelle
*Sauvignon Blanc,
Columbia Valley*

Columbia Crest
*Two Vines Merlot-Cabernet,
Columbia Valley*

GABRIELLA'S VEGETABLE RISOTTO

The godfather of my son Dominic has a niece who lives in Croatia. She makes this wonderful side dish to accompany grilled fish. You can use chicken broth, if you are not a total vegetarian.

1 quart vegetable or chicken broth
¼ cup olive oil
1 yellow onion, diced small
3 cloves garlic, mashed
1 cup grated zucchini or ½ cup each
   grated zucchini and yellow squash

¼ cup chopped fresh Italian parsley
1 tablespoon fresh thyme
¼ cup Sauvignon Blanc
2 cups Arborio rice
Salt, to taste
Parmesan cheese, for serving

Bring the broth to a boil in a saucepan; reduce heat and keep hot until needed.

Heat the olive oil in a heavy saucepan over medium heat. Sauté the onion and garlic in oil until soft. Add the grated squash and continue to sauté until the squash is soft. Stir in the parsley and thyme. Add the wine and simmer for 5 minutes. Add the rice and stir until the liquid is absorbed. Add about ½ cup of the hot broth to the rice. Continue to stir until the rice absorbs the broth. Repeat this until rice is al dente. Season with salt to taste. Serve with a generous amount of Parmesan cheese.

WINE
RECOMMENDATIONS:

COLUMBIA CREST
*Grand Estates Pinot Grigio,
Columbia Valley*

OR

*Two Vines Riesling,
Columbia Valley*

GREAT NORTHERN BEAN CASSEROLE

1 pound Great Northern beans
2 tablespoon olive oil
2 small yellow onions, chopped
4 cloves garlic, chopped
¼ cup celery tops, chopped
1 cup Roma tomatoes, chopped
1 quart vegetable stock

¼ cup Sauvignon Blanc
3 tablespoon chopped fresh Italian
   parsley
3 tablespoons chopped fresh oregano
1 teaspoon ground cumin
Pinch red pepper flakes
Salt, to taste

Add 3 quarts of water to a large pot. Pour in the beans and boil for 10 minutes. Turn off heat; cover and let stand for 1 hour.

Heat a large heavy-gauge pot to medium-hot, add olive oil. Sauté onion, garlic, and celery until soft.

Reduce heat to medium. Add tomatoes and cook until very soft. Add vegetable stock, wine, parsley, oregano, cumin, and pepper flakes. Drain the beans and add them to the broth. Salt to taste. Cover and simmer over low heat, stirring occasionally, for 1½ hours, or until beans are very tender.

I love this dish in the wintertime. Good bread, and romaine salad dressed with olive oil and vinegar, and a bottle of red are all you need for a gratifying cold-weather meal. This may be served as a hearty casserole, or with additional broth it becomes a rich soup.

WINE
RECOMMENDATIONS:

CHATEAU STE. MICHELLE
*Cabernet Sauvignon,
Columbia Valley*

SPRING VALLEY VINEYARD
*Nina Lee Syrah,
Walla Walla Valley*

Porcini Mushroom Pasta

Mushroom admirers will appreciate this pasta dish. Porcini, with their meat-like texture, lend themselves to countless recipes. If you haven't yet fully utilized this king of mushrooms, then here's a great recipe to inspire your culinary mastery.

FOR PASTA:

1 pound fettuccine or pappardelle
  noodles

FOR PORCINI MUSHROOM SAUCE:

2 tablespoons olive oil

2 tablespoons butter

2 large yellow onions, julienned

2 cloves garlic, mashed

2 cups veal or chicken stock

¼ cup Sauvignon Blanc

1 cup rehydrated porcini mushrooms,
  with juice

1 tablespoon chopped fresh Italian
  parsley

1 tablespoon chopped fresh thyme

Pinch cumin

Salt, to taste

Black pepper, to taste

FOR GARNISH:

Chopped fresh tomato

Chopped fresh basil

Parmesan cheese

TO PREPARE PASTA: Boil water in a large stockpot over high heat. Add pasta to the boiling water and cook according to package directions, about 8 to 10 minutes. Drain.

TO PREPARE SAUCE: Heat oil and butter in a large skillet. Sauté onion and garlic until very soft, about 10 minutes. Stir in stock, wine, mushrooms with their juice, parsley, thyme, and cumin. Simmer until slightly thicken. Season with salt and pepper to taste.

TO SERVE: Pour the sauce over the hot cooked pasta. Garnish with tomato, basil, and Parmesan cheese.

WINE
RECOMMENDATIONS:

COLUMBIA CREST
*Grand Estates Shiraz,
Columbia Valley*

OR

*Grand Estates Pinot Grigio,
Columbia Valley*

"Shrooms on a Shingle" in Chardonnay Cream Sauce

Chef Kurt Olson, Chateau Ste. Michelle Winery

FOR SHINGLE:

3 slices of brioche, crusts removed, cut in half on an angle

1 tablespoon butter, melted

FOR MUSHROOMS:

3 tablespoons olive oil, divided

1 medium shallot, diced

1 clove garlic, minced

1 cup Chardonnay

1 cup vegetable stock

2 cups heavy cream

1 pound wild mushrooms (chanterelle, lobster, morels, porcini), mixed or single variety, cleaned and sliced into ⅓-inch pieces.

2 tablespoons sherry

2 teaspoons lemon juice

1 teaspoons thyme, chopped

Salt, to taste

Black pepper, to taste

FOR SERVING:

6 thyme sprigs

Parmesan cheese, shaved

TO PREPARE SHINGLE: Brush brioche with butter, place on a baking sheet and bake at 350°F for approximately 7 minutes, until golden brown.

TO PREPARE MUSHROOMS: In a small sauce pot over medium heat, add 1 tablespoon of olive oil and sweat the shallots and garlic for 1 minute. Add the wine, reduce to 1 ounce. Add the vegetable stock, reduce to 1 ounce. Add the cream, reduce by half. Strain and keep warm. This can be done up to 2 hours in advance.

Heat a sauté pan over high heat, add 2 tablespoons of olive oil and the mushrooms. Sauté for 3 to 4 minutes. Add the sherry, cook until almost all the liquid has evaporated. Add the cream sauce, bring to a boil then reduce the heat. Season the sauce with the lemon juice, thyme, salt, and pepper.

TO SERVE: Place brioche in serving bowls with chanterelle cream. Garnish with a sprig of thyme and some shaved Parmesan.

The term "shingle" comes from the Army— if you were in the military, then you know what this means.

WINE RECOMMENDATIONS:

Chateau Ste. Michelle
Ethos Reserve Chardonnay, Columbia Valley

Erath
Oregon Pinot Noir

Spinach Lasagna

My boys love this dish and they hate spinach. The portobello mushrooms will provide a meaty texture for vegetarians who seek that characteristic.

FOR SAUCE:

2 tablespoons olive oil

2 large onions, chopped

6 cloves garlic, chopped

¼ cup celery leaves, chopped

4 cups chopped Roma tomatoes

⅛ cup Sauvignon Blanc

1 cup vegetable stock

2 tablespoons chopped fresh Italian
  parsley

2 tablespoons chopped fresh basil

2 tablespoons chopped fresh oregano

¼ cup chopped sun-dried tomatoes

Pinch sugar

Salt, to taste

Black pepper, to taste

FOR LASAGNA:

8 sheets lasagna pasta

½ pound portobello mushrooms, sliced

Sauce (recipe above)

2 bunches fresh spinach, cleaned and
  stemmed

1½ pounds fresh mozzarella cheese, sliced

½ cup freshly grated Parmesan cheese,
  for top

TO PREPARE SAUCE: Sauté onions in the oil until soft. Add garlic and celery and sauté 3 more minutes. Add tomatoes and simmer until very soft, 10 to 15 minutes. Add wine, vegetable stock, parsley, basil, oregano, sun-dried tomatoes, and sugar. Season with salt and pepper to taste. Simmer for 30 minutes. Set aside to cool.

TO PREPARE LASAGNA: Preheat oven to 350°F.

In a large stockpot, bring water to a rolling boil. Add pasta and cook just to al dente, according to package directions; do not cook through. Drain and lay flat.

In a skillet, briefly sauté mushrooms.

In an 8- by 8-inch or 9- by 9-inch baking dish or pan, pour a scoop of sauce on the bottom and spread evenly. Place 2 lasagna noodles on sauce, and spread another scoop of sauce over pasta. Place a thin layer of spinach leaves, mushrooms, then mozzarella cheese. Add more sauce. Repeat layering with 2 more layers of pasta, spinach, mushrooms, cheese, and sauce. Finish the top layer with pasta, sauce, and mozzarella cheese. Sprinkle with freshly grated Parmesan cheese and bake in oven for 60 minutes or until sauce is bubbling and hot.

WINE
RECOMMENDATIONS:

ERATH
Oregon Pinot Gris

OR

COLUMBIA CREST
*Grand Estates
Cabernet Sauvignon,
Columbia Valley*

ᴏ⌇ Mᴇᴀᴛ ⌇ᴏ

ARGENTINE-STYLE MIXED GRILL

Typically an Argentine grill has a combination of meat, fowl, and even organ meats. You can mix and match different cuts of meat together to your liking. This can be prepared a day ahead and marinated overnight. Serve mixed grill with a tossed green salad and good crusty French bread.

FOR CHIMICHURRI:

1 cup chopped Italian parsley

1 cup olive oil

2 tablespoons chopped fresh oregano

½ cup chopped sweet roasted red pepper

1 medium yellow onion, diced

6 cloves garlic, chopped fine

⅛ cup red wine vinegar

1 tablespoon salt

Pinch red pepper flakes

FOR MEAT:

½ pound flank steak or strip steak

1 (1-pound or less) pork tenderloin

2 small chickens, quail, or game hens, halved

¼ cup Cabernet Sauvignon

FOR GARNISH:

2 lemons, cut into wedges

TO PREPARE CHIMICHURRI: Mix all ingredients together.

TO PREPARE MEAT: Spoon about ¼ cup of the chimichurri over the steak, pork, and fowl; rub gently. Sprinkle the meat and fowl with the wine and toss together. Let marinate at least 1 hour or overnight.

Preheat an outdoor grill on medium heat.

Grill the fowl and pork until both are cooked through; then grill the steak to medium-rare.

TO SERVE: Slice the steak, pork, and fowl and place on a platter. Spoon more of the chimichurri over the meats. Serve with the lemon wedges.

WINE
RECOMMENDATIONS:

COLUMBIA CREST
Reserve Cabernet Sauvignon,
Columbia Valley

CHATEAU STE. MICHELLE
Syrah,
Columbia Valley

Asian Honey-Spiced Ribs

2 tablespoons peanut oil

1 small yellow onion, grated

3 cloves garlic, minced

1 tablespoon grated fresh ginger

½ cup soy sauce

⅔ cup chicken stock

¼ cup Merlot

1 teaspoon dry mustard

2 tablespoons honey

2 tablespoons chopped fresh cilantro

2 tablespoons tomato paste

½ teaspoon Asian sesame oil

¼ teaspoon hot chili oil

3 pounds beef or pork ribs

Salt, to taste

Freshly ground black pepper, to taste

Heat a skillet over medium-high heat. Add the peanut oil and, when hot, add the onion, garlic, and ginger. Cook until the onions are soft, about 5 minutes. Add the soy sauce, chicken stock, wine, dry mustard, honey cilantro, tomato paste, sesame oil, and chili oil and simmer until thickened, about 20 minutes.

Meanwhile, preheat the oven to 450°F.

Place the ribs on a baking sheet and sprinkle with salt and pepper. Roast the ribs in the oven for about 20 minutes, turning once, to brown both sides. Reduce the heat to 350°F. Baste the ribs generously with the marinade; cover with aluminum foil and bake for 30 minutes. Turn and baste again. Cover the ribs again with foil and bake an additional 30 to 50 minutes, basting occasionally, until the ribs are fork-tender.

Asian foods are especially hard to match with red wine, but try a fruit-forward red such as a Washington Merlot or Syrah or a California Zinfandel.

WINE
RECOMMENDATIONS:

COLUMBIA CREST
H3 Merlot,
Horse Heaven Hills

SNOQUALMIE
Syrah,
Columbia Valley

VILLA MT. EDEN
Zinfandel,
California

BRAISED BEEF CHEEKS

Beef cheeks and pork cheeks are back in style. You can use either in this recipe. Serve with oven-roasted and mashed fall root vegetables and baby broccoli.

3 pounds beef cheeks
½ cup flour, for dredging
2 tablespoons olive oil
2 tablespoons butter
1 large yellow onion, julienned
2 carrots, diced
2 stalks celery, diced
3 cloves garlic, finely chopped
2 tablespoon chopped fresh Italian

3 sprigs fresh rosemary
3 sprigs fresh thyme
1 bay leaf
2 tablespoon Dijon mustard
1 cup Cabernet Sauvignon
½ cup beef stock
1 teaspoon salt
½ teaspoon pepper

Dredge the beef cheeks in flour. Heat the olive oil and butter in a heavy Dutch oven over medium-high heat. Brown the cheeks well on both sides. Remove and keep warm. Add the onion, carrot, celery, and garlic. Sauté until soft. Add the remaining ingredients and bring to a simmer. Return the cheeks to the pot and cover.

Bake in the oven at 300°F for 90 minutes, turning every ½ hour, until the cheeks are fork tender. Remove from the oven; remove beef cheeks and keep warm. Strain the sauce from the pot and let settle. Skim off the excess oil.

Pour the sauce into a saucepan. Bring to a slow simmer and reduce to thicken. To help thicken the sauce, make a paste by mixing ½ cup beef broth into 2 tablespoons flour. Mix into the sauce, stirring constantly, until thick.

To serve, place the cheeks on a serving plate and spoon sauce over them.

WINE
RECOMMENDATIONS:

STAG'S LEAP WINE CELLARS
*S.L.V. Estate
Cabernet Sauvignon,
Napa Valley*

OR
*ARTIMIS Napa Valley
Cabernet Sauvignon,
Napa Valley*

BRAISED LAMB SHANKS IN SYRAH WITH POLENTA

FOR LAMB SHANKS:

2 tablespoons olive oil

4 lamb shanks (have the butcher trim the bone)

Salt, to taste

Black pepper, to taste

Flour, for dredging

2 medium onions, julienned

1 fennel bulb, julienned

4 cloves garlic, mashed

2 carrots, shredded

1 tablespoon tomato paste

1 tablespoon freshly chopped rosemary

1 tablespoon freshly chopped thyme

1 tablespoon freshly chopped Italian parsley

1 bay leaf

½ cup Syrah

½ cup beef stock, plus more if needed

FOR POLENTA:

6 cups chicken broth, divided

1 teaspoon salt

1 cup medium polenta

2 tablespoons butter

Freshly ground black pepper

¼ cup freshly grated Parmesan cheese

TO PREPARE LAMB SHANKS: Heat the olive oil to medium-high in an oven-proof, covered heavy pot or high-sided skillet. Season shanks with salt and pepper and dredge in flour. Place the shanks into the pot and brown well on all sides. Remove the shanks from the pot. Add the onion, fennel, and garlic. Sauté the vegetables until soft. Stir in the carrot and tomato paste. Add the rosemary, thyme, parsley, and bay leaf. Stir in the wine and stock. Return the lamb to the pot.

Bake, covered, in the oven at 300°F for 90 minutes total, turning often. Remove the lid for the last 30 minutes to allow caramelizing. If the lamb needs more liquid, add stock, not wine or water. The meat should fall off the bone when done.

TO PREPARE POLENTA: Pour 3 cups of the broth into a large heavy pot. Add the salt and stir in the polenta. Bring to a boil over high heat, stirring constantly.

In a separate pot, bring 3 more cups of the broth to a boil. Reduce to simmer; cover and keep hot.

Reduce the heat for the polenta and simmer, stirring every few minutes, until thickened, about 10 minutes. Add additional hot broth, 1 cup at a time as needed, and continue to cook over low heat. Cook, stirring frequently to prevent sticking and scorching. Cook until soft and creamy, this can take between 20 and 40 minutes. Stir in the butter, season with black pepper, and the Parmesan cheese.

My favorite way to serve this dish is to spoon the polenta onto individual serving plates then top the polenta with the lamb meat and the caramelized vegetables with their gravy. To top it all off, boil some green peas in a saucepan and spoon these on to the dish for color and flavor.

WINE RECOMMENDATIONS:

SPRING VALLEY VINEYARD
*Uriah Red Wine,
Walla Walla Valley*

OR

*Nina Lee Syrah,
Walla Walla Valley*

Braised Rabbit with Pinot Noir and Dried Cherries

This is a recipe my Bubba (grandma) would make. Serve with your choice of pappardelle pasta or gnocchi.

FOR RABBIT:

1 fresh rabbit cut into 8 pieces (like a chicken, the butcher could do this)

Salt, to taste

Black pepper, to taste

2 tablespoons olive oil

2 pieces bacon

1 yellow onion, julienned

4 cloves garlic, finely chopped

6 shallots, halved

2 celery ribs, diced

3 Roma tomato, diced

1 tablespoon tomato paste

1 tablespoon chopped fresh rosemary

2 tablespoons chopped fresh Italian parsley

1 cup Pinot Noir

½ cup chicken stock

Scant ⅛ teaspoon fresh grated nutmeg

½ cup dried cherries

FOR PASTA:

½ pound pappardelle pasta or gnocchi

FOR GARNISH:

Freshly grated Parmesan cheese

Freshly chopped parsley

TO PREPARE RABBIT: Season the rabbit with the salt and pepper and set aside. Heat the olive oil in large, covered heavy pot and fry bacon until crisp. Remove the bacon, coarsely crumble, and set aside. Brown the rabbit in the pot on all sides; remove rabbit pieces. Add the onion, garlic, shallots, and celery. Sauté the vegetables until soft. Stir in the tomato, rosemary, parsley, wine, stock, and nutmeg. Bring to a simmer. Place the bacon and rabbit back into the pot; cover.

Cook in the oven at 325°F or on top of the stove on low heat. After 30 minutes, remove the loin and keep warm; turn the other pieces. Add the dried cherries. Cover and continue cooking for a further 30 minutes. Remove the cover and continue cooking to let the sauce reduce, about 10 minutes.

TO PREPARE PASTA: Bring water to a boil in a large stockpot. Add the pasta or gnocchi and cook according to package directions.

TO SERVE: Place the pasta or gnocchi on a platter. Arrange the rabbit on top of the pasta and spoon sauce over the pasta and rabbit. Garnish with the Parmesan cheese and chopped parsley.

WINE RECOMMENDATIONS:

ERATH
Estate Selection Pinot Noir, Dundee Hills

NORTHSTAR
Merlot, Columbia Valley

GRILLED LAMB CHOPS PROVENÇAL

FOR MARINADE:

2 tablespoons olive oil

1 tablespoons Dijon mustard

¼ cup Syrah

1 teaspoon chopped fresh parsley

1 teaspoon chopped fresh basil

1 teaspoon chopped fresh rosemary

1 teaspoon chopped fresh thyme

½ teaspoon chopped fresh lavender

Pinch salt

Generous amount fresh ground black
  pepper

FOR LAMB:

4 double cut (2 rib) lamb chops

TO PREPARE MARINADE: Mix all the ingredients together in a small bowl.

TO PREPARE LAMB: Rub the marinade over the lamb chops. Let marinate at least 1 hour or preferably over night.

    Preheat an outdoor grill on medium heat.

    Grill the lamb over medium heat, about 3 minutes per side, until medium rare.

I like to serve this succulent lamb with ratatouille and buttered fettuccine.

WINE
RECOMMENDATIONS:

COLUMBIA CREST
*Grand Estates Shiraz,
Columbia Valley*

CHATEAU STE. MICHELLE
*Canoe Ridge Estate Merlot,
Horse Heaven Hills*

STAG'S LEAP WINE CELLARS
*ARTEMIS Napa Valley
Cabernet Sauvigon,
California*

Herbed Leg of Lamb with Sweet Cherry Sauce

You wouldn't think it could be so simple to make this mouth-watering leg of lamb.

FOR HERB MIXTURE:

⅛ cup extra virgin olive oil

6 cloves garlic, finely chopped

2 tablespoons finely chopped fresh rosemary

2 tablespoons finely chopped Italian parsley

1 teaspoon black pepper

⅛ cup Merlot

Pinch salt

FOR LAMB:

1 bone-in leg of lamb

FOR SWEET CHERRY SAUCE:

3 tablespoon butter

3 large shallots, thinly sliced

1 tablespoon flour

1 cup beef or veal stock

⅓ cup Syrah or Merlot

1 tablespoon chopped fresh rosemary

⅛ teaspoon grated fresh nutmeg

Salt, to taste

1 cup pitted cherries

TO PREPARE HERB MIXTURE: Mix all the ingredients together in a small bowl.

TO PREPARE LAMB: Preheat the oven to 350°F.

Make a small incision into the leg of lamb every 2 inches, about 1½-inches deep. Stuff each incision with some of the herb mixture.

Rub the remaining herb mixture over lamb and let stand 1 hour.

Bake on a rack for 1½ hours or until medium rare.

TO PREPARE SWEET CHERRY SAUCE: Melt the butter in a sauté pan over medium-low heat and slowly sauté the shallots until soft.

Sprinkle in the flour and stir to incorporate the flour with the shallots.

Add the stock, wine, rosemary, nutmeg, and salt. Bring to a simmer. Add the cherries and simmer until soft, about 5 minutes.

WINE RECOMMENDATIONS:

NORTHSTAR
Merlot,
Columbia Valley

CONN CREEK
ANTHOLOGY,
Napa Valley Red Wine

Herbed Tenderloin of Beef

FOR MARINADE:

1 tablespoon chopped fresh thyme

1 tablespoon chopped fresh rosemary

2 cloves garlic, mashed

4 teaspoons Dijon mustard

2 tablespoons olive oil

¼ cup Merlot

½ teaspoon salt

½ teaspoon black pepper

FOR BEEF:

1 (3- to 4-pound) tenderloin

TO PREPARE MARINADE: Mix all the ingredients in a small bowl.

TO PREPARE BEEF: Place the beef tenderloin into a baking dish. Rub marinade over entire tenderloin. Let marinate 1 hour at room temperature.

Preheat the oven to 400°F.

Bake in the oven, about 15 minutes per pound, until rare to medium-rare; inner temperature of 120°F to 125°F on a meat thermometer.

By using this wet rub as a marinade you will create a tender and delicious roast tenderloin of beef. If you would like, you can marinate this over night in the refrigerator.

WINE
RECOMMENDATIONS:

COL SOLARE
Red Wine,
Columbia Valley

SPRING VALLEY VINEYARD
Frederick Cabernet Sauvignon,
Walla Walla Valley

CONN CREEK
Cabernet Sauvignon,
Napa Valley

Korean-Style Beef Skewers

Top sirloin, flank steak, or skirt steak will all work well for this recipe.

FOR MARINADE:

½ cup soy sauce

¼ cup Syrah

2 teaspoons peeled grated ginger

3 cloves garlic, mashed

1 tablespoon tomato paste

1 tablespoon honey

1 tablespoon vegetable oil

1 teaspoon sesame oil

FOR BEEF:

1½ pounds top sirloin, cut into strips   ½-inch wide by 3- to 4-inches long

FOR GARNISH:

Chopped fresh cilantro

TO PREPARE MARINADE: Mix all the ingredients together in a small bowl.

TO PREPARE BEEF: Marinate the steak for at least 1 hour or overnight.

Preheat an outdoor grill on hot heat.

Soak the bamboo skewers in water for 30 minutes. Skewer the marinated meat. Grill on the hot grill until cooked medium-rare, about 3 minutes per side.

TO SERVE: Remove the beef skewers to a serving platter and garnish with the chopped cilantro.

WINE
RECOMMENDATIONS:

CHATEAU STE. MICHELLE
Merlot,
Columbia Valley

COLUMBIA CREST
Two Vines Shiraz,
Columbia Valley

Little Birds with Fettuccine

FOR STUFFING:

2 cloves garlic, mashed

4 ounces pancetta, chopped

8 chopped pimento-stuffed green olives

1 tablespoon chopped fresh Italian
  parsley

¼ cup Asiago Cheese

⅓ cup bread crumbs

⅓ cup extra virgin olive oil

Pinch salt

Pinch black pepper

FOR BEEF:

2 pounds top round roast
  or top round veal

2 tablespoons olive oil

FOR SAUCE:

1 large yellow onion, diced

2 cloves garlic, mashed

1 large (28-ounce) can fresh tomatoes
  in puree

¼ cup Cabernet Sauvignon

⅛ teaspoon allspice

Pinch sugar

Pinch salt

Pinch black pepper

FOR GARNISH:

½ cup cooked green peas

½ cup chopped fresh basil

TO PREPARE STUFFING: Mix all the stuffing ingredients together thoroughly.

TO PREPARE BEEF : Cut beef into ¼-inch-thick rounds. Under wax paper,
pound the beef until thin.

    Place a spoonful of the stuffing in the center of the beef. Roll up and secure
with toothpicks. Heat the olive oil in a high-sided saucepan on medium heat.
Brown the beef on all sides. Remove from the pan.

TO PREPARE SAUCE: Add the onion and garlic to the same pan. Sauté for several minutes or until the vegetables are soft. Add the remaining sauce ingredients:
tomatoes in puree, wine, allspice, sugar, salt, and pepper. Simmer for 30 minutes.

TO SERVE: Add the beef rolls back into the pan. Cover and simmer for 20 minutes. When cooked, transfer to a warm serving dish. Sprinkle with peas and basil.

*In parts of Italy, where
this dish comes from,
when the beef is rolled and
tied it looks to them like
little nesting birds. Italians
call many dishes little:
"little huts," "little pillows,"
"little beans," "little ears."*

WINE
RECOMMENDATIONS:

CONN CREEK
*ANTHOLOGY,
Napa Valley Red Wine*

CONN CREEK
*Cabernet Sauvignon,
Napa Valley*

Flat Iron Steak

Flat iron steak is a rich and relatively tender piece of beef. Its rectangular shape and uniform thickness makes it an ideal steak for the grill. If you are unable to locate this cut of beef, ask your butcher for top blade steak instead.

FOR MARINADE:

2 tablespoons olive oil

2 cloves garlic, mashed

1 teaspoon chopped fresh Italian parsley

1 teaspoon chopped fresh rosemary

¼ cup Cabernet Sauvignon

½ teaspoon dry mustard

Pinch salt

Generous amount freshly ground black pepper

FOR STEAKS:

2 (1-pound) flat iron steaks or 1 (2-pound) flank steak

TO PREPARE MARINADE: Mix all marinade ingredients in a large dish.

TO PREPARE STEAKS: Place the steaks into the marinade and marinate for 1 hour, turning occasionally.

Grill the steaks over high to medium-high heat, 4 minutes per side. This steak is best cooked rare to medium-rare.

Wine
Recommendations:

Columbia Crest
*Walter Clore Private Reserve Red Wine,
Columbia Valley*

Columbia Crest
*Grand Estates
Cabernet Sauvignon,
Columbia Valley*

GRILLED PORK TENDERLOIN WITH WHITE BEAN RAGU

This is Italian "pork and beans." It's great with Col Solare from Washington or with the red wines of Tuscany. I served this meal at Col Solare's grand opening celebration.

FOR PORK:

2 tablespoons olive oil

1 tablespoon lemon juice

¼ cup white wine

2 tablespoons chopped fresh Italian parsley

1 tablespoon chopped fresh thyme

3 cloves garlic, mashed

1 tablespon Dijon mustard

Pinch salt

Pinch black pepper

FOR BEANS:

2 tablespoons olive oil

⅛ cup chopped pancetta

2 cloves garlic, chopped

1 red onion, diced

2 Roma tomatoes, diced

4 sage leaves

⅛ teaspoon cumin

¼ cup chicken broth

2 (10-ounce) cans small white beans, rinsed and drained

FOR SERVING:

1 tablespoon olive oil

2 tablespoons red wine vinegar

1 bunch arugula

2 tablespoons chopped fresh basil

2 tablespoons chopped fresh Italian parsley

TO PREPARE PORK: Mix all ingredients except pork until blended. Pour over pork and let marinate for 1 hour.

Preheat an outdoor grill on medium heat.

Grill pork over medium heat until temperature reaches 160°F. Do not overcook.

TO PREPARE BEANS: Heat olive oil in sauté pan over medium heat. Sauté the pancetta, garlic, and onion in the oil until soft. Add the tomatoes, sage, cumin, and stock. Bring to a simmer. Add the beans. Cook until most of the moisture has reduced.

TO SERVE: Mix together the red wine vinegar and olive oil. Toss arugula with the olive oil and vinegar dressing until well coated. Place dressed arugula onto a large platter. Spoon the beans onto the platter with the arugula. Slice the pork and arrange on top. Garnish with freshly chopped basil and parsley.

WINE
RECOMMENDATIONS:

COL SOLARE
Red Wine,
Columbia Valley

NORTHSTAR
Merlot,
Columbia Valley

LAMB CHOPS WITH RATATOUILLE AND NOISETTE POTATOES

This flavorful combination of meat, vegetables, and potatoes makes a terrific meal. Ratatouille is a classic dish. The noisette potatoes are easy and complete the presentation.

FOR LAMB STOCK:

2 tablespoons olive oil

1 pound lamb trimmings

2 large onions, thickly sliced

2 stalks celery, cut into 1-inch chunks

2 carrots, cut into 1-inch pieces

1 tablespoon tomato paste

½ cup red wine

1 tablespoon chopped fresh rosemary

1 tablespoon chopped fresh thyme

2 bay leaves

4 cloves garlic, coarsely chopped

6 peppercorns

2 cups veal stock

FOR SAUCE:

3 tablespoons butter, divided

3 shallots, finely chopped

2 cloves garlic, finely chopped

½ cup red wine

1 tablespoon chopped fresh thyme

1 cup lamb stock (recipe above)

⅛ teaspoon salt

⅛ teaspooon black pepper

FOR LAMB CHOPS:

2 tablespoons olive oil

8 lamb chops

2 cloves garlic, mashed

1 tablespoon chopped fresh thyme

⅛ teaspoon salt

⅛ teaspoon black pepper

FOR RATATOUILLE:

⅓ cup olive oil

1 onion, diced

2 cloves garlic, chopped

1 red bell pepper, diced

1 yellow bell pepper, diced

1 green bell pepper, diced

1 zucchini, diced

1 eggplant, diced

2 tablespoons tomato paste

1 bouquet garni

2 tomatoes, concassé

Basil, cut into thin ribbons

Salt, to taste

Black pepper, to taste

FOR NOISETTE POTATOES:

3 russet potatoes

2 tablespoons butter

FOR SERVING:

2 tablespoons olive oil

4 basil leaves

8 tomato skins

4 sprigs thyme

WINE RECOMMENDATIONS:

COL SOLARE
Red Wine,
Columbia Valley

NORTHSTAR
Merlot,
Columbia Valley

TO PREPARE STOCK: Sear the lamb trimmings in oil, then add the onions, celery and carrots and continue to sear until well browned. Add the tomato paste and red wine and reduce until almost evaporated. Add the rosemary, thyme, bay leaves, garlic cloves, peppercorns, and the veal stock, and simmer for 1 hour over low heat. Skim any fat and impurities that rise to the surface. Strain and reserve.

TO PREPARE SAUCE: Sweat the shallots and garlic in 2 tablespoons butter. Add the red wine and thyme and reduce until the liquid is evaporated. Add the lamb stock. Cook until reduced by one quarter. Strain the sauce through a fine sieve and return to the pan. Whisk in 1 tablespoon butter. Adjust the seasonings to taste. Keep the sauce hot.

TO PREPARE LAMB CHOPS: Marinate the lamb chops with olive oil, garlic, thyme, salt, and pepper for several hours. Sear the lamb chops in a hot skillet on both sides and cook to desired degrees of doneness, remove the chops and let them rest for a couple of minutes.

TO PREPARE RATATOUILLE: Sauté the onions and garlic in olive oil, until soft. Add the peppers, zucchini, and eggplant and cook for 5 minutes until the vegetables are almost tender. Add the tomato paste and bouquet garni. Cook for another 5 minutes. Add the tomatoes and fresh basil. Season with salt and pepper to taste. Set aside.

TO PREPARE POTATOES: Preheat oven to 400°F. Scoop small balls from the potatoes to make 12 potato balls. Heat the butter over high heat in skillet. Place the potato balls in the pan and shake to coat with butter; cook until golden brown.

Transfer the potatoes to a baking tray and place in oven. Bake for about 20 minutes, until soft and cooked through.

TO SERVE: Heat olive oil in a frying pan until very hot. Fry the basil leaves and tomato skins in oil until crisp, about 1 minute. Place on a paper towel to drain. Spoon the ratatouille into the center of a serving platter and arrange the chops around it. Accompany with noisette potatoes and the sauce. Garnish with thyme sprig, crisp basil leaf, and crisp tomato skins.

Marinated Rack-of-Lamb

This rack-of-lamb will be its most delicious when it is left to marinade overnight.

FOR MARINADE:

2 tablespoons olive oil

1 tablespoon balsamic vinegar

2 tablespoons red wine such as Zinfandel or Merlot

2 tablespoons Dijon mustard

2 cloves of garlic, mashed

1 bay leaf, crushed

1 tablespoon chopped fresh Italian parsley

1 tablespoon chopped fresh rosemary

1 tablespoon chopped fresh thyme

Pinch salt

Pinch black pepper

FOR LAMB:

2 lamb racks (have the butcher "French" them—cut the excess fat off ribs and back)

TO PREPARE MARINADE: Mix all the marinade ingredients together in a large zip-lock bag.

TO PREPARE LAMB: Add the lamb racks to the bag and rub the marinade around the meat. Refrigerate overnight.

Preheat an outdoor grill on medium heat or the oven to 325°F.

Roast lamb in the oven, about 15 minutes, or grill, about 7 minutes per side, until meat is cooked rare. Insert a meat thermometer so the tip is not touching bone or fat. The meat thermometer will register 140°F (60°C) for rare.

WINE
RECOMMENDATIONS:

CHATEAU STE. MICHELLE
*Ethos Reserve Merlot,
Columbia Valley*

STAG'S LEAP WINE CELLARS
*Cask 23 Estate
Cabernet Sauvignon,
Napa Valley*

Pizza Siciliano

FOR PIZZA DOUGH:

4 cups flour

½ teaspoon salt

1 teaspoon instant yeast

¼ cup olive oil

1½ cups ice cold water

FOR MARINARA SAUCE:

¼ cup olive oil

4 cups peeled, seeded, and finely
    chopped Roma tomatoes

Pinch pepper flakes

Pinch salt

Pinch sugar

FOR TOPPING:

1 cup marinara sauce (recipe above)

¼ pound prosciutto, thinly sliced

⅓ cup crumbled Gorgonzola cheese

½ cup halved fresh figs

¼ cup chopped fresh basil

¼ cup chopped fresh arugula

TO PREPARE PIZZA CRUST: Mix together the flour, salt, and yeast. Stir in the oil and water, until the flour has absorbed the liquid. This can be done in a food processor or a mixer using the hook accessory. Mix the dough gently until it comes away from the sides of the bowl. You may need to add more flour.

Divide the dough into 4 pieces. Roll each piece into a ball and place on an oiled sheet pan. Cover with a damp cloth and refrigerate for at least 2 hours or overnight.

Preheat the oven to 500°F. Dust a cutting board with flour and roll out the dough to the desired thickness. Bake on a pizza stone in hot oven for 2 to 3 minutes.

TO PREPARE MARINARA SAUCE: Heat the olive oil in a heavy saucepan over low heat. Add the tomatoes. Stir in the pepper flakes, salt, and sugar. Heat the sauce until just barely simmering. Do not allow the sauce to boil as this will make it taste bitter. Cook until thickened and reduced by at least half, about 20 to 25 minutes, stirring occasionally to break up the tomatoes.

TO TOP PIZZA: Spread the marinara sauce over the prebaked crust. Lay a few slices of the prosciutto around the pizza and sprinkle with the Gorgonzola. Add the figs. Place the pizza back into the oven just long enough to melt the cheese, about 3 to 5 minutes. Remove from the oven and sprinkle with chopped basil and arugula.

For an authentic Siciliano pizza, roll this crust thinly; I think the thinner the better. I like to serve this with olives and green onions on the side.

WINE
RECOMMENDATIONS:

COL SOLARE
*Red Wine,
Columbia Valley*

SNOQUALMIE
*Naked Merlot,
Columbia Valley*

CHATEAU STE. MICHELLE
*Cabernet Sauvignon,
Columbia Valley*

PORK TENDERLOIN WITH RAISINS AND OREGON HAZELNUTS

The rich flavor of this sauce can in part be credited to the humble little hazelnut that is added right at the end. Tender pieces of pork are quickly browned and smothered in a seasoned sauce. It's downright delicious.

¼ cup raisins

¼ cup red wine

2 large pork tenderloins (about 1½ pounds total)

½ cup flour

½ teaspoon salt

½ teaspoon finely ground black pepper

2 tablespoons olive oil

1 yellow onion, thinly sliced

2 shallots, finely chopped

1 clove garlic, chopped

¼ cup Dry Riesling

⅛ teaspoon dry mustard

1 teaspoon chopped fresh Italian parsley

1 teaspoon chopped fresh thyme

Pinch cayenne pepper

Pinch grated lemon zest

1 tablespoon balsamic vinegar

2 tablespoons chopped roasted hazelnuts

Parsley sprigs, for garnish

Soak raisins in red wine vinegar for about 20 minutes.

Cut pork tenderloins into ¾-inch slices and gently pound to about ½-inch thickness.

Mix flour, salt, and pepper; dredge pork in seasoned flour. Add olive oil to a hot, heavy skillet. Quickly brown pork on both sides; remove to warm platter.

Sauté onion, shallots and garlic in the same pan until just soft, do not brown. Stir in wine. Add drained raisins, mustard, parsley, thyme, cayenne pepper, lemon zest, vinegar, and hazelnuts; stir until well combined. Simmer for 2 to 3 minutes, until sauce thickens.

Spoon sauce over pork and garnish with sprigs of parsley.

WINE RECOMMENDATIONS:

ERATH
Estate Selection Pinot Noir, Dundee Hills

COLUMBIA CREST
H3 Chardonnay, Horse Heaven Hills

Pork Tenderloin with Apples, Green Chiles, and Calvados

FOR PORK:

2 pork tenderloins (about 1½ pounds total)

1 tablespoon olive oil

½ teaspoon chili powder

Juice of 1 lime

2 cloves garlic

1 tablespoon chopped fresh cilantro

1 teaspoon chopped fresh thyme

½ teaspoon salt

¼ teaspoon black pepper

FOR SAUCE :

2 tablespoons olive oil

3 tablespoons bacon, chopped

1 large green Granny Smith or Pippin apple, cut into 1/2-inch cubes

1 large yellow onion, finely chopped

1 (4-ounce) can whole green chiles, thinly sliced

⅛ cup Dry Riesling

1 teaspoon chopped cilantro

1 teaspoon dry mustard

1 teaspoon chili powder

1 ounce Calvados brandy

1 to 2 tablespoons brown sugar

Salt, to taste

TO PREPARE PORK: Mix together all ingredients and rub over the pork. Let stand about 1 hour.

Preheat an outdoor grill on medium heat.

Grill meat over medium heat until done, about 7 minutes per side.

TO PREPARE SAUCE: Heat oil in sauté pan over medium-high heat. Sauté bacon in oil until soft. Add apple and onion; sauté quickly until wilted. Add remaining ingredients and stir until blended together.

TO SERVE: Arrange the pork on a platter and pour sauce over tenderloins.

Delicious—and with the addition of Calvados, it's a little exotic. Produced in the Calvados region of Northern France, this premium apple brandy enhances the flavor of meat and fruit dishes.

WINE RECOMMENDATIONS:

CHATEAU STE. MICHELLE & DR. LOOSEN
*Eroica Riesling,
Columbia Valley*

OR

*Indian Wells Merlot,
Columbia Valley*

Rib Eye Steak and Figs Grilled over Grapevines with Cabernet Pan Sauce & Arugula-Walnut Salad

Chef Kim Marshall, Chateau Ste. Michelle Winery

Two words—complexity and interest—go a long way in describing the Cabernet Pan Sauce. There's a moment of culinary bliss that happens with your first mouthful of this combination meal that includes tender steak, grilled fresh figs, and Gorgonzola.

3 (1-pound) boneless rib eye steaks, about 1½-inches thick

2 strips bacon, diced

4 cloves garlic, minced

2 large pinches dried thyme

1 bay leaf

½ small onion, finely diced

Coarse salt, to taste

Freshly ground black pepper, to taste

1 teaspoon tomato paste

2 cups Cabernet Sauvignon

2 cups rich chicken stock

16 figs, halved, and tossed with 1 teaspoon extra virgin olive oil

6 tablespoon unsalted butter, room temperature

4 to 5 ounces baby arugula

½ cup toasted walnuts

4 ounces Gorgonzola

2 tablespoons aged balsamic vinegar

4 tablespoons extra virgin olive oil

Remove steaks from from the refrigerator, and allow them to reach room temperature. Fire up a charcoal or wood-fire grill.

Plunge a few handfuls of grapevine cuttings in water to soak for about 30 minutes.

Cook the bacon until crisp in a medium saucepan over medium heat; quickly strain the excess fat and return the pot to the stove. Add the garlic, thyme, and bay leaf; sauté until fragrant, about 20 seconds. Stir in the onion, a pinch of salt, and pepper; continue to cook until golden brown, about 5 minutes. Stir in the tomato paste; cook for another 20 seconds. Slowly pour in the wine, stirring to deglaze the pan. Increase heat to medium-high and bring the sauce to a boil; reduce heat to medium and simmer until liquid is reduced to ½ cup. Stir in the chicken stock; cook until the liquid is reduced again to about ½ cup. Set aside until ready to serve. Note: at this point, sauce can be stored in the refrigerator for up to 2 days.

When the charcoal is covered with a whitish ash, scatter soaked grapevine cuttings around the coals and set the grill grate in place (a few inches above coals).

Season the steaks with salt and pepper and place on grill; cook 4 minutes. Rotate 90° and cook another 3 minutes. Flip the steaks over and repeat the process until cooked to desired doneness. Transfer the steaks to plate, loosely cover with foil and set aside to rest a few minutes.

Wine Recommendations:

Chateau Ste. Michelle
*Artist Series Meritage Red Wine,
Columbia Valley*

Chateau Ste. Michelle
*Ethos Reserve Cabernet Sauvignon,
Columbia Valley*

Season the figs with a pinch of salt and quickly grill, cut-side down, until marked. Transfer to a small plate and set aside.

Bring the sauce to a boil, whisk in the butter and season to taste with salt and pepper; set aside. Slice the steaks against the grain and arrange on a serving platter. Drizzle with the pan sauce and top with the figs.

Toss together in a medium bowl, the arugula, walnuts, and Gorgonzola with a pinch of salt, balsamic vinegar, and olive oil. Serve with the steak.

ROASTED VEAL CROATIAN-STYLE

Croatian meals are simply created with fresh ingredients. The flavors of the meat, vegetables, and seasonings combine and enhance each other. This creates a tasty meal that is greater than the sum of its parts.

1 (3- to 4-pound) veal shoulder roast, cut into 6 pieces
4 onions, quartered
2 red peppers, quartered
2 yellow bell peppers, quartered
6 potatoes, quartered

4 whole garlic bulbs, trimmed
1 tablespoon chopped fresh sage
½ teaspoon salt
½ teaspoon black pepper
½ cup extra virgin olive oil

Preheat the oven to 400°F.

Place the meat, onions, peppers, potatoes, and garlic into a Dutch oven. Sprinkle with the sage, salt, and pepper. Drizzle the olive oil over the meat and vegetables and then mix well to coat thoroughly.

Cover the dish and bake in the oven for 30 minutes. Remove from the oven and turn the vegetables and the meat. Cover and cook another 30 minutes.

WINE RECOMMENDATIONS:

COLUMBIA CREST
*Reserve Syrah,
Columbia Valley*

CHATEAU STE. MICHELLE
*Horse Heaven Vineyard
Sauvignon Blanc,
Horse Heaven Hills*

STEWED BEEF BORDEAUX-STYLE

FOR STEWED BEEF:

3 pounds beef chuck steak or chuck
   roast, cut into 1½-inch pieces

Flour, for dredging

Salt

Pepper

1 tablespoon olive oil

1 tablespoon butter

1 large onion, chopped

3 Roma tomatoes, chopped

2 carrots, chopped

1 cup pearl onions

1 tablespoon tomato paste

1 tablespoon Dijon mustard

1 teaspoon chopped fresh rosemary

1 teaspoon chopped fresh thyme

1 bay leaf

2 cups red wine

1 cup beef stock

1 cup sliced fresh mushrooms (any
   variety or a mixture)

2 tablespoons butter

FOR POTATOES:

4 large baking potatoes

3 tablespoons butter

⅓ cup milk or cream

2 tablespoons horseradish

This recipe includes mashed potatoes but you could serve this stew with noodles instead. Just before serving, add cooked extra-wide egg noodles on top with a little fresh chopped Italian parsley.

TO PREPARE STEWED BEEF: Preheat the oven to 325°F.

   Dredge the beef in flour seasoned with salt and pepper. Brown the beef in the olive oil and butter until well browned. Remove from pot and keep warm. Add to the pot the onion, tomato, carrots, and pearl onions and sauté until tender. Then add the tomato paste, mustard, rosemary, thyme and bay leaf. Stir well. Add the wine and the stock. Season with salt to taste. Return the beef to the pot; cover and cook in oven for 30 minutes. After 30 minutes, stir the stew; cover and cook another 30 minutes. Stir and cook, covered, another 30 minutes, for 1½ hours total, or until beef is very tender.

   While the beef is cooking, sauté the mushrooms in the butter, until soft. When the beef is tender, stir them into the mushrooms.

TO PREPARE POTATOES: Peel the potatoes and boil in salted water until tender. Drain the potatoes and add the butter and milk or cream. Mash and add the horseradish.

WINE
RECOMMENDATIONS:

COL SOLARE
Red Wine,
Columbia Valley

CONN CREEK
ANTHOLOGY,
Napa Valley Red Wine

NORTHSTAR
Walla Walla Valley Merlot

VEAL CHOPS

After browning, the veal chops are kept moist and tender by cooking in a beautiful liquid at a low temperature.

FOR MARINADE:

⅛ cup olive oil

Juice of ½ lemon

⅛ cup Chardonnay

Splash Worcestershire sauce (white if available)

2 tablespoons chopped fresh Italian parsley

1 tablespoon chopped fresh thyme

1 teaspoon dry mustard

2 cloves garlic, chopped

½ teaspoon salt

¼ teaspoon black pepper

FOR VEAL:

4 veal chops (with bone in)

Flour. for dredging

2 tablespoons (¼ stick) butter

2 tablespoons olive oil

TO PREPARE MARINADE: Mix together all ingredients until well combined.

TO PREPARE VEAL: Marinate the veal chops for 1 hour. Pat dry with paper towel. Lightly flour.

Preheat oven to 275°F.

Heat butter and oil in a sauté pan over medium-high heat. Brown chops on both sides until very golden brown. Remove to a platter and place in preheated oven for approximately 20 minutes. To the same pan, add remaining marinade and quickly reduce.

TO SERVE: Spoon the sauce over the veal chops.

WINE RECOMMENDATIONS:

CHATEAU STE. MICHELLE
Cold Creek Vineyard Chardonnay, Columbia Valley

STAG'S LEAP WINE CELLARS
ARCADIA VINEYARD Chardonnay, Napa Valley

❧ SIDE DISHES ❧

BABY BROCCOLI SAUTÉ

Baby broccoli has a tender texture and a milder, sweeter taste than broccoli. You can find it in specialty food stores and many supermarkets.

1 pound baby broccoli
3 tablespoons olive oil
2 cloves garlic, chopped
1 tablespoon red wine vinegar

⅛ teaspoon salt
Grated fresh Parmesan cheese, for garnish

Boil water in a medium saucepan with 1 teaspoon salt added. Add the baby broccoli and blanch for 3 minutes. Drain and rinse with cold water.

Heat the olive oil in a sauté pan over medium heat. Sauté the garlic until soft. Add the baby broccoli, vinegar, and salt and sauté for about 9 minutes.

Place on plate and garnish with Parmesan cheese.

BRUSSELS SPROUTS WITH PANCETTA AND SHALLOTS

With a flavorful balsamic glaze, this recipe might even convert those who have bad memories of Brussels sprouts. For the best flavor keep the Brussels sprouts crisp. Over-cooking is what brings out the strong taste and smell that many dislike.

2 dozen Brussels sprouts
1 teaspoon salt
2 tablespoons olive oil
4 slices pancetta, chopped
2 large shallots, thinly sliced

2 cloves of garlic, mashed or chopped
2 tablespoons red wine vinegar
Salt, to taste
Black pepper, to taste

Bring water to a boil in a medium saucepan, add salt and parboil the Brussels sprouts for 2 minutes. Drain. Heat the olive oil in a skillet over medium high and sauté the pancetta, shallots, and garlic, until the pancetta is crispy and the shallots and garlic are lightly brown. Add the vinegar. Simmer for 2 minutes. Add the Brussels sprouts. Simmer over low heat for 5 minutes. Season with salt and pepper to taste.

GREEN BEANS AND POTATOES

6 medium red potatoes

1 quart chicken stock or water

3 fresh sage leaves

1 clove garlic, mashed

½ teaspoon salt

1 pound fresh green beans, halved

⅛ cup olive oil

Freshly ground black pepper

Boil the potatoes in stock or water with the sage leaves, garlic clove, and salt until just about cooked through. Add the green beans; cover, and cook until beans are tender, not crunchy. Drain the liquid. Add the olive oil. Season with black pepper to taste. Mix thoroughly. The potatoes should break apart a little and become a bit mashed.

The common potato becomes extraordinary with the addition of fresh beans and staple ingredients. Serve with steak for a sophisticated meat and potatoes meal.

ONION, SWEET PEPPER, AND FENNEL ROASTED "SALAD"

A roasted salad is a good accompaniment for grilled chicken breasts or pork tenderloin.

2 yellow onions, thickly julienned

2 red bell peppers, thickly julienned

2 yellow bell peppers, thickly julienned

2 fennel bulbs, thickly julienned

4 cloves garlic, thinly sliced

3 tablespoons olive oil

1 teaspoon chopped fresh thyme

1 teaspoon salt

½ teaspoon black pepper

Preheat the oven to 350°F.

Toss together all the vegetables, oil, and thyme until the vegetables are well coated. Spread the vegetables out in a shallow roasting pan. Season with salt and pepper.

Roast in the oven for 45 minutes, turning frequently.

Pan-Roasted Peppers and Onions

2 tablespoons olive oil

1 large red bell pepper, julienned

1 large yellow bell pepper, julienned

1 large yellow onion, julienned

2 cloves garlic, thinly sliced

1 teaspoon balsamic vinegar

Salt, to taste

Heat the olive oil in a skillet over medium heat. Slowly sauté the bell peppers, onions, and garlic, stirring frequently until the vegetables are soft, about 20 minutes. Increase the heat slightly and lightly brown, watching so they do not burn. Add the balsamic vinegar and season with salt to taste. Lower the heat and cook another 5 minutes.

This delicious combination goes very well with sausage or lamb, and would be nice served with polenta.

Potatoes, Peppers, and Onions

6 yellow potatoes, cut into wedges

1 large red bell pepper, thickly sliced

1 large yellow bell pepper, thickly sliced

1 yellow or red onion, quartered and separated

3 cloves garlic, halved

¼ cup olive oil

2 tablespoons balsamic vinegar

2 teaspoons freshly chopped oregano

Salt

Freshly ground black pepper

Preheat oven to 450°F.

Combine the potatoes, peppers, onions, and garlic in a shallow roasting pan. Mix together the olive oil, balsamic vinegar, and oregano. Drizzle the oil mixture over the vegetables and toss until vegetables are completely coated. Season with salt and pepper. Bake the vegetables in the roasting pan for about 30 minutes, turning occasionally.

Oven-roasting the vegetables retains their flavor and nutrition. It could also be made with seasonal vegetables such as butternut squash or sweet potatoes.

ROASTED-GARLIC WHIPPED POTATOES

8 medium potatoes

1 whole garlic bulb, roasted
  (see page 222)

¼ cup olive oil

1 teaspoon freshly chopped basil

Salt, to taste

Black pepper, to taste

Bring the potatoes to a boil in a large saucepan of salted water. Cook until tender and easily pierced with a fork, about 10 to 15 minutes. Drain and transfer to a bowl.

Squeeze the roasted garlic into the potatoes. Add the olive oil and basil. Season with salt and pepper to taste. Whip the potatoes with an electric mixer until fluffy.

Spicy White Beans

2 cups small white beans

1 cup chopped Roma tomatoes

½ cup chopped green onions

2 cloves garlic, chopped

1 tablespoon chopped fresh basil

1 tablespoon chopped fresh parsley

1 tablespoon chopped fresh oregano

1 tablespoon capers

1 anchovy fillet, chopped

2 tablespoons olive oil

1 tablespoon balsamic vinegar

Pinch red pepper flakes, or to taste

Salt, to taste

Black pepper, to taste

Bring beans and 4 cups water to boil; boil 2 minutes. Remove from heat and let beans soak 1 hour. Return to heat and let simmer for 1 to 1½ hours, until beans are tender. Drain and set aside to cool.

Mix together all remaining ingredients in a medium-size bowl. Add beans and toss together until well combined. Season with salt and pepper to taste.

This dish can be prepared ahead of time and kept in the refrigerator until ready to serve. It nicely complements pork tenderloin.

Stuffed Tomatoes

4 large tomatoes

1 cup fine bread crumbs

¼ cup grated Parmesan cheese

1 clove garlic, minced

1 tablespoon chopped parsley

1 tablespoon chopped basil

⅛ cup olive oil

1 tablespoon soft butter

Pinch salt

Pinch black pepper

Preheat oven to 350°F.

Cut the tomatoes in half through the middle and remove the inner flesh and seeds. Mix together all other ingredients. Spoon the mixture into the hollowed out tomatoes. Place in a baking dish and bake for 10 minutes.

This warm tasty treat is easier to prepare than you may think.

POLENTA

Polenta is a staple food in the Mediterranean, and especially in North Italy. Its versatility makes polenta a great side dish, whether served at an everyday supper or a festive banquet.

6 cups chicken broth, divided
1 teaspoon salt
1 cup medium polenta

2 tablespoons butter
Freshly ground black pepper
¼ cup freshly grated Parmesan cheese

Pour 3 cups of the broth into a large heavy pot. Add the salt and stir in the polenta. Bring to a boil over high heat, stirring constantly.

In a separate pot, bring 3 more cups of the broth to a boil. Reduce to simmer; cover and keep hot.

Reduce the heat for the polenta and simmer, stirring every few minutes, until thickened, about 10 minutes. Add additional hot broth, 1 cup at a time as needed, and continue to cook over low heat. Cook, stirring frequently to prevent sticking and scorching. Cook until soft and creamy, this can take between 20 and 40 minutes. Stir in the butter, season with black pepper, and the Parmesan cheese; remove from heat.

POLENTA WITH ROASTED GARLIC AND PARMESAN CHEESE

2½ cups chicken broth

1 cup polenta

1 whole garlic bulb, roasted (see page 222)

½ cup grated Parmesan cheese

1 tablespoon butter

½ cup heavy cream

Pinch salt

Bring the chicken broth to a simmer in a heavy saucepan over medium-high heat. Add the polenta and stir or whisk constantly for 15 minutes. Add the roasted garlic, Parmesan, butter, cream, and salt. Simmer for about 5 more minutes, continuing to stir.

Pour into a 6- by 8-inch baking dish and chill until firm, about 4 hours or overnight.

Remove from the dish and cut into wedges. May be grilled on the barbecue, for about 3 to 4 minutes each side, or until grill marks form. Alternatively, it can be baked in a preheated 350°F oven for about 10 to 15 minutes.

Homemade polenta is much, much better than what you can buy premade in a store. Polenta is versatile and can be served with many different foods.

RISI E BISI (RICE AND PEAS)

This creamy risotto is a Venetian classic that is traditionally made with freshly harvested sweet baby peas.

2 cups chicken broth

2 tablespoons olive oil

1 large yellow onion, chopped thin

⅛ cup chopped celery leaves

2 cloves garlic, mashed

¼ cup Sauvignon Blanc

1½ cups uncooked short-grain rice, such as Arborio or Carnaroli

2 tablespoons chopped Italian parsley

½ cup grated Parmesan cheese

1 (6-ounce) package frozen or 1½ cups fresh baby peas

Bring the chicken stock to a boil in a covered saucepan. Reduce the heat to low, cover, and simmer until needed.

Heat the olive oil in a skillet on medium-high heat. Sauté the onion, celery, and garlic, until the vegetables are very soft, about 4 to 6 minutes. Add the wine and rice. Cook over medium-high heat, stirring, until rice absorbs liquid, about 2 minutes. Using a ladle, slowly add simmering broth 1 ladle at a time. Stir and boil for 2 minutes. Reduce heat to low, cover, and cook until the rice is tender, about 15 minutes. Add the peas and cook 2 to 4 minutes longer, until the peas are heated through.

Stir in the parsley and Parmesan cheese.

SAFFRON-LEMON RICE

1 teaspoon peanut oil

¼ teaspoon peeled grated fresh ginger

1 clove garlic, mashed

1 small yellow onion, chopped

Pinch saffron

¼ teaspoon lemon zest

2 cups chicken stock

¼ cup Chardonnay

1 cup long grain or Basmati rice

½ teaspoon salt

Heat the oil over medium heat in a 4-quart saucepan. Sauté the ginger, garlic, and onion until soft. Add the saffron, lemon zest, chicken stock, and wine. Bring to a boil. Add the rice and reduce heat to simmer. Cover and cook for 10 minutes. Remove from heat and stir. Season with salt to taste. Let stand, covered, for 15 minutes, to cook the rice through.

Lemon-flavored rice is a natural balance for fish and seafood. It also goes wonderfully with main dishes such as meat skewers, Greek lamb, or roast chicken.

Agliata Garlic Sauce

Agliata garlic sauce dates back to the Middle Ages. The full flavor and intense aroma enhance simple dishes such as pasta, and light meats like chicken, veal or pork. It can be tossed with vegetables like steamed fresh green beans. I also recommend serving it over Croatian Calamari on page 92.

1 large loaf day-old French bread, crust removed, cut in 1-inch cubes
4 teaspoons white wine vinegar
2 teaspoons water
4 cloves garlic, mashed
1 cup olive oil

2 tablespoons chopped fresh basil
1 tablespoon chopped fresh Italian parsley
Pinch salt
Pinch white pepper

Mix the bread, vinegar, water, and garlic with a fork until pasty. Add olive oil a little at a time until the mixture is smooth. Add basil, parsley, salt, and pepper.

Roasted Garlic

Roasted garlic has a mild sweet flavor. It's simple to do and great for enjoying with Brie, spreading on French bread, or mixing into potatoes or pasta.

1 whole bulb garlic
Olive oil, to taste

Pinch salt
Pinch black pepper

Remove the dry outer peels from the garlic. Cut about ½-inch off the top of the garlic bulb exposing the cloves. Drizzle some olive oil over the garlic and rub the oil into the bulb with your fingers. Season with salt and pepper. Wrap the entire bulb in foil and place in the oven to cook until soft, about 45 minutes. The garlic will steam and cook inside the foil.

Squeeze the bulb to remove the soft garlic. Use as a spread or mash with fork for use in recipes.

SICILIAN MARINARA SAUCE

¼ cup olive oil

4 cups peeled, seeded, and finely
   chopped Roma tomatoes

3 cloves garlic, thinly sliced

½ cup chicken stock

¼ cup white wine

Pinch pepper flakes

Pinch salt

Pinch sugar

Heat olive oil in a heavy saucepan over low heat. Add tomatoes and garlic. Add chicken stock and wine. Stir in pepper flakes, salt, and sugar. Heat until just barely simmering. Do not allow sauce to boil as this will make it taste bitter. Cook until thickened and reduced by at least half, about 20 to 25 minutes, stirring occasionally to break up tomatoes.

It's easy to keep all the ingredients on hand for this standard, versatile marinara sauce. Homemade is so much better than store-bought sauce. Quality canned tomatoes can be substituted in a pinch. Once made, this marinara sauce can be used for several recipes in this book, including Sicilian Seafood Pasta and Eggplant Zucchini Strata.

WHOLE-BERRY CRANBERRY TWIST

The flavor of this cranberry sauce is best when made a day ahead. Serve Cranberry Twist with Sausage-Stuffed Fresh Roast Turkey on page 174.

1 (16-ounce) can whole cranberry sauce

2 tablespoons blackberry jam (or other jam of choice)

¼ teaspoon peeled grated fresh ginger

⅓ cup diced red onion

½ cup freshly squeezed orange juice

Mix all ingredients in a bowl. Chill.

❧ Desserts ❧

Apple Strudel
with Dried Cherries and Raisins

For me, this is a comfort food on the dessert menu. You can adjust the proportions of dried cherries and raisins to suit your preferences.

¼ cup dried cherries

¼ cup golden raisins

½ cup brandy

¼ cup chopped hazelnuts

⅛ teaspoon cinnamon

Pinch nutmeg

⅛ teaspoon orange zest

¼ cup brown sugar

2 tablespoons white sugar

⅛ cup flour

4 Granny Smith apples (or other tart apples), peeled, cored, and sliced

1 package fillo dough or strudel dough

2 tablespoons butter, melted

Whipped cream or ice cream, for serving

Fresh berries, for garnish

Mint sprig, for garnish

Soak the dried cherries and raisins in the brandy until soft, about 20 minutes.

In a large mixing bowl, mix together the hazelnuts, cinnamon, nutmeg, orange zest, brown sugar, white sugar, and flour. Drain the soaked fruit and stir into the other ingredients in the bowl. Add the apples and toss.

Preheat the oven to 350°F.

Lay a sheet of fillo or strudel dough on a lightly greased baking sheet and lightly brush with the clarified butter. Repeat this to have 5 layers.

Place the apple mixture in the middle of the rectangle of dough and fold over ends. Roll up to form a log. Butter the outside of the strudel and bake in a preheated oven until golden brown, about 20 minutes. (Alternatively, after buttering the sheets and placing the filling, cut the sheets into equal portions, either squares or strips that can be rolled. Lay onto baking sheet. Butter the edges and bake in preheated oven until golden brown.)

Serve with whipped cream or ice cream, and garnish with berries and mint sprig if desired.

Wine
Recommendations:

Chateau Ste. Michelle
*Ethos Reserve Late Harvest
White Riesling,
Columbia Valley*

or

*Late Harvest Riesling,
Washington State*

Warm Berries over Ice Cream

For me, dessert and dessert-style wine aren't always a perfect match. A dessert wine is dessert all by itself. But for those with a sweet tooth who want to serve wine, here is a simple dessert that will pair well with Late Harvest Riesling.

FOR BERRIES:

1 cup strawberries

1 cup blueberries

1 cup raspberries

1 tablespoon honey

1 teaspoon balsamic vinegar

Pinch orange zest

FOR SERVING:

Vanilla ice cream

Biscotti

TO PREPARE BERRIES: Place the berries in a small pot over medium heat. Add the honey, balsamic vinegar, and orange zest. Bring just to a simmer and cook until the berries are softened.

TO SERVE: Spoon the berry mixture over a good-quality vanilla ice cream and serve with biscotti.

WINE
RECOMMENDATION:

CHATEAU STE. MICHELLE
*Ethos Reserve
Late Harvest White Riesling,
Columbia Valley*

Chocolate Mousse with Cabernet Syrup

Executive Chef Janet Hedstrom, Chateau Ste. Michelle Winery

There are so many good things to say about Chocolate Mousse: it makes an elegant dessert, you can prepare individual presentations, and it can be prepared a day ahead. This version, made with Cabernet Syrup, only needs one word to describe it— exquisite!

FOR CABERNET SYRUP:

1 cup Cabernet Sauvignon	¾ cup sugar

FOR CHOCOLATE MOUSSE:

4 ounces bittersweet chocolate, finely chopped	½ cup red wine syrup (recipe above)
6 ounces semi-sweet chocolate, finely chopped	3 tablespoons water
	1½ cups heavy cream
3 tablespoons unsalted butter, cut into small pieces	1 tablespoon vanilla extract
	2 tablespoons sugar
	3 egg yolks

FOR CRUMB BASE:

1 package dark chocolate wafer cookies	3 tablespoons butter, melted

FOR CHOCOLATE TOPPING:

½ cup (1 stick) butter	2 tablespoons heavy cream
1 cup semi-sweet chocolate chips	

TO PREPARE SYRUP: Place the wine and sugar in a heavy bottom saucepan. Bring to a boil over high heat and then reduce the heat to a simmer. Cook for 5 minutes, remove from the heat and cool. This makes enough for 2 batches.

TO PREPARE MOUSSE: Place the chocolates, butter, ½ cup of wine syrup, and water in a medium-sized bowl over a pan of barely simmering water, so the bowl does not touch the water. (Or place in the top of a double boiler over gently boiling water.) Stir the chocolate mixture often until completely melted, being careful not to overheat the chocolate. Remove the chocolate from the heat and cool slightly.

Whip the cream with the vanilla and sugar to form soft peaks; set aside. Whisk the egg yolks into the chocolate mixture until completely blended. Then gently fold in the whipped cream until just mixed. Refrigerate for at least 1 hour before serving.

TO PREPARE CRUMB BASE: Process cookies in a food processor or blender until fine crumbs. Drizzle in the butter and mix.

TO SERVE: Melt butter and chocolate together in a small saucepan over medium heat. Stir until combined; stir in the cream. Allow to cool completely. Press crumb mixture into molds. Spoon in the mousse to about 1/4-inch from the top. Top with the melted chocolate mixture and refrigerate at least 1 hour or overnight.

APPLE AND PEAR COMPOTE

This is best served warm with a good-quality vanilla bean ice cream. You don't always need wine with dessert, as often a dessert wine is dessert. Sometimes a good cup of coffee will end the meal nicely.

3 apples, peeled, cored, and cut into thin wedges

3 pears, peeled, cored, and cut into thin wedges

1 tablespoon lemon juice

2 tablespoons butter

2 tablespoons sugar

½ teaspoon cinnamon

½ teaspoon nutmeg

¼ cup Late Harvest Riesling

½ teaspoon orange zest

Sprinkle the apples and pears with the lemon juice as soon as possible after slicing. Melt the butter in a large sauté pan over medium heat. Add the apple and pear slices and sauté for 3 to 5 minutes, until fruit begins to soften. Add the sugar, cinnamon, nutmeg, wine, and orange zest. Simmer for 5 minutes. Remove from heat. Serve over vanilla ice cream while still warm.

WINE
RECOMMENDATIONS:

*Ice Wine or
Late Harvest Riesling,
Washington State*

APPLE AND PEAR TARTE TATIN

3 green apples

3 firm pears

1 ounce butter

1 cup brown sugar, not packed

Zest of 1 orange

½ cup Late Harvest Riesling

Pinch of cinnamon

Pinch of nutmeg or mace

Pie dough or puff pastry

1 tablespoon melted butter or 1 egg
blended with 1 tablespoon of water

1 cup heavy cream, whipped

Peel and core the apples and pears and cut into quarters.

Preheat the oven to 350°F.

Combine the butter and brown sugar in a 10-inch nonstick tart pan or fry pan that can be transferred to the oven. Heat over medium-high, stirring constantly, until smooth. Add the zest and wine; reduce, stirring constantly, to make the caramel sauce. Stir in the cinnamon and nutmeg; remove from heat.

Place the apples and pears into a pan, alternating them for a pretty pattern, round-side down. Return to heat; simmer, covered, for 5 minutes to soften the fruit.

Roll out the dough. If using puff pastry, roll fairly thinly so it does not get too puffed while baking. Cut into 10-inch circle. Top the apples and pears with the dough round. Lightly brush the top with melted butter or egg. Place the tart into the oven and bake for about 20 minutes, or until the dough is golden brown. Remove the tart and let cool for a few minutes.

While still warm, place a plate or serving platter over the pan and turn the tart over onto the plate. Serve warm, topped with whipped cream.

I prefer Newtown Pippin apples for this recipe, if you are able to find them. They are tart, firm, and excellent for pies. Tart, crisp Granny Smith apples are also very good.

WINE
RECOMMENDATION:

SNOQUALMIE
*Winemaker's Select Riesling,
Columbia Valley*

APPLE-BERRY COBBLER

This is delicious with a combination of fresh berries or just your favorite berry. To complete this dessert, simply enjoy with vanilla ice cream or crème fraîche.

FOR DOUGH:

1 cup flour	⅛ teaspoon salt
¼ cup sugar	6 tablespoons butter (¾ stick), cubed
1 tablespoon baking powder	¾ cup cream

FOR FILLING:

1½ pounds apples, sliced	⅓ cup sugar
½ pound berries (choose from black-berries, raspberries, blueberries)	¼ teaspoon cinnamon
	¼ teaspoon cardamom

FOR SERVING:

Ice cream or crème fraîche

TO PREPARE DOUGH: Mix the flour, sugar, baking powder, and salt in a medium bowl. Add the butter and mix to a coarse cornmeal consistency. Add the cream and mix just until combined. Pull the dough together to form a ball; flatten slightly and refrigerate. When ready to use, roll out the dough to fit the baking dish

TO PREPARE FILLING: Mix all the filling ingredients together in a large bowl. Place the filling in a shallow baking dish. Place the rolled dough on top. Bake about 30 minutes, or until the dough is golden brown.

FOR SERVING: Serve in bowls, accompanied by a scoop of ice cream or a dollop of crème fraîche.

WINE
RECOMMENDATION:

DOMAINE STE. MICHELLE
*Extra Dry Sparkling Wine,
Columbia Valley*

APPLES FILLED AND BAKED WITH LATE HARVEST WHITE RIESLING

2 apples, peeled and cut in half
¼ cup golden raisins
¼ cup chopped hazelnuts or walnuts
¼ cup firmly packed brown sugar

2 tablespoons unsalted butter, softened
½ cup plus 1 tablespoon Late Harvest
   White Riesling
½ cup water

Preheat oven to 350°F.

Scoop out the center of each apple half, forming a small cup to hold the filling.

Mix together the raisins, nuts, brown sugar, butter and 1 tablespoon of the Riesling. Spoon an equal amount of filling into each apple half.

Place the apples in a nonreactive baking dish fitted with a lid. Pour the water and the ½ cup of Riesling around the bottom of the apples.

Cover and bake for 30 minutes, or until apples are tender when pierced with a fork. Uncover the apples and bake 5 to 10 minutes more, until tops are golden.

Warm from the oven, these fragrant baked apples fill the house with a wonderful spicy aroma. Large, firm apples with a tart flavor, such as Granny Smiths, work best. To prevent discoloration, soak the peeled apples in a mixture of lemon juice and cold water.

WINE
RECOMMENDATION:

CHATEAU STE. MICHELLE
*Ethos Reserve Late Harvest
White Riesling,
Columbia Valley*

Apple Custard Mousse with Cherries

*This mousse makes
a wonderful dessert
presentation when served
with both toppings, but
it can also be served
with either the sweet
apple purée or the cherry
topping instead of both.*

FOR MOUSSE:

1¼ cups milk

½ cup sugar

6 egg yolks

¼ cup cold water

1 tablespoon gelatin

1 cup whipping cream

1 tablespoon apple brandy (Calvados)

FOR SWEET APPLE PURÉE:

2 medium apples, peeled, cored, and
  thinly sliced (Braeburn, Jonathan, or
  Golden Delicious)

1 tablespoon lemon juice

½ cup sugar

¼ cup Late Harvest White Riesling

FOR CHERRY TOPPING:

1 cup water

1 cup Port wine

½ cup sugar

¼ cup packed brown sugar

1 tablespoon grated orange zest

1 cinnamon stick

1 tablespoon cornstarch, mixed with 1
  tablespoon water

4 cups pitted sweet cherries (frozen or
  canned)

TO PREPARE MOUSSE: Warm the milk in a saucepan over medium heat until
bubbles begin to form around the outside. Add the sugar and stir until dissolved.

Whisk the egg yolks lightly in a medium bowl. Add 3 tablespoons of the
sugared milk to yolks, whisking constantly. Pour the egg mixture into milk and
stir until smooth. Cook until the mixture coats a spoon, stirring constantly, about
7 minutes.

Pour the cold water into a small bowl, sprinkle in the gelatin and soften for 5
minutes. Stir the dissolved gelatin into the warm custard. Place the saucepan with
the custard over a bowl of ice and chill in the refrigerator.

Whip the cream until firm. Stir the apple brandy into the whipped cream.
When the custard begins to firm, fold in the whipped cream. Pour into a buttered
mold. Chill for 6 hours.

TO PREPARE SWEET APPLE PURÉE: Blend the apples, lemon juice, sugar, and
Riesling in a blender or food processor.

WINE
RECOMMENDATIONS:

CHATEAU STE. MICHELLE
*Ethos Reserve Late Harvest
White Riesling,
Columbia Valley*
OR
*Muscat Canelli,
Columbia Valley*

TO PREPARE CHERRY TOPPING: Bring the water to a boil in a large saucepan then add the wine, sugar, brown sugar, orange zest, and cinnamon. Return to a boil and continue to boil slowly for 3 minutes. Blend cornstarch with 1 tablespoon water and stir into the boiling sugar water. Cook, stirring constantly, until thickened. Remove cinnamon stick. Stir in the cherries.

TO SERVE: Assemble by first unmolding the mousse. Then top the mousse with the sweet apple purée and cherry topping.

Fruit Salad

2 cups cubed watermelon

1 pint strawberries, halved

½ small pineapple, cubed

1 teaspoon lemon juice

1 teaspoon lime juice

2 teaspoons chopped fresh mint

Toss all the ingredients together. Serve chilled.

For me, a good dessert doesn't need to be laden with sugar. This is a simple, refreshing, and healthy completion.

FIGS AND BALSAMIC SYRUP

The pleasure of fresh figs has been largely lost for most—this tantalizing recipe should remedy that. This little luxury can be used as a starter course or a dessert; plan on two to three figs per person. Less expensive balsamic vinegar can be used, as it will sweeten when reduced.

Fig lovers rejoice!

1 cup balsamic vinegar
⅓ cup Syrah
2 tablespoons orange juice

8 to 12 fresh figs (depending on size)
2 to 3 slices prosciutto, each cut into 4
    strips

Heat the balsamic vinegar, wine, and orange juice over low heat in a small saucepan. Cook over medium heat until thickened and reduced by half.

To serve, wrap the figs with the prosciutto. Place on serving plates and spoon balsamic syrup over the top.

Lemon Sorbet

1 cup water

1 cup sugar

½ cup lemon juice

Zest of 1 whole lemon, plus additional
  for garnish (optional)

⅓ cup Late Harvest Riesling

Mint sprigs, for garnish (optional)

Bring the water to a boil in a medium saucepan. Add the sugar, lemon juice, and lemon zest. Simmer, stirring often, until the sugar is completely dissolved, about 10 minutes. Stir in the wine. Let cool.

To freeze, use an ice cream maker and process as directed by the manufacturer; without an ice cream maker, spoon the mixture into a shallow pan and freeze, for about 8 hours, or overnight, until firm.

Garnish with a few strands of lemon zest and a sprig of mint if desired.

Note: To make Italian gelato, allow the lemon mixture to cool. Stir in 1 cup of half-and-half to the lemon mixture. It is best if you have an ice cream maker to freeze the gelato.

Lemon sorbet is ideal for perking up the appetite and refreshing the palate between courses. It also makes a refreshing, intensely flavorful dessert. Other citrus fruit sorbets and gelatos can be made the same way— simply substitute lime or orange juice.

Orange-Infused Olive Oil Cake with Fresh Fruit and Raspberry Coulis

Chef Regina Paul-Jones, Chateau Ste. Michelle Winery

This is a classic dessert for the crew at Chateau Ste. Michelle. Olive oil produces a wonderfully moist cake, and oranges give this cake its zing! People might be tentative to try an olive oil cake, but all reservations will end when they take their first bites.

FOR OLIVE OIL CAKE:

3 eggs

2 cups sugar

Zest of 3 oranges (washed, dried, and finely grated)

1¼ cups milk

1¼ cups olive oil

¼ teaspoon vanilla

2¼ cups all purpose flour

1 tablespoon baking powder

Pinch salt

FOR COULIS:

12 ounces frozen raspberries

¾ cup sugar

1 tablespoon lemon juice

1 tablespoon cornstarch

1½ tablespoons water or Late Harvest Semillon

FOR SERVING:

1 tablespoon powdered sugar

3 cups raspberry coulis (recipe above)

6 cups berries or fresh fruit such as peaches, nectarines, cherries

Whipped cream, slightly sweetened

TO PREPARE OLIVE OIL CAKE: Preheat the oven to 350°F.

Spray two 8-inch spring form pans and line the bottom with parchment. Place the eggs and sugar in the bowl of an electric mixer and beat until light and thick, about 5 minutes. Add the orange zest, milk, oil, and vanilla. Beat just until smooth, do not over mix. Combine the flour, baking powder, and salt in a bowl, then sift onto the egg mixture. Gently fold to combine. Pour the batter into the prepared baking pans and bake until tester inserted into the center comes out clean, about 45 minutes. Cool the cake completely in the pan on a rack.

TO PREPARE COULIS: Thaw the berries and purée with the sugar and lemon. Whisk together the cornstarch and water. Place the strained juice into a pan and bring to a boil. Whisk in the cornstarch mixture and boil for 1 minute. Remove from heat. Place the pan in ice water and continue whisking until cool.

TO SERVE: Cut the cake into 12 pieces and sift powdered sugar over the top. Place 1 ounce of the berry coulis on each plate. Lay a piece of cake on top of the coulis, garnish with ½ cup of fruit, and top with the whipped cream.

WINE RECOMMENDATION:

CHATEAU STE. MICHELLE *Late Harvest Chenin Blanc, Columbia Valley*

OREGON BLUEBERRY TART WITH HAZELNUT TOPPING

FOR TART DOUGH:

2 cups flour   1 cup butter

¼ cup sugar   1 egg

FOR FILLING:

2 cups fresh blueberries, divided   1 teaspoon lemon zest

½ cup sugar   ⅛ teaspoon cinnamon

¼ cup flour

FOR TOPPING:

2 cups blueberries   1 cup hazelnuts

¼ cup sugar

A fresh blueberry tart such as this could be considered unpretentious baking, but the addition of roasted hazelnuts swings it toward a trendy restaurant dessert.

TO PREPARE DOUGH: Combine the flour, sugar, and butter in a food processor and mix until the butter is fully incorporated. Add the egg and mix until dough comes together in a ball. On a floured work surface, roll out the dough to fit an 11-inch tart pan. Chill for at least 30 minutes.

TO PREPARE FILLING: Toss the blueberries with the sugar, flour, lemon zest, and cinnamon.

TO PREPARE TOPPING: Preheat the oven to 325°F.

Roast the hazelnuts in preheated oven for about 5 minutes until lightly browned. Rub hazelnuts in a kitchen towel to remove skins. Crush into small pieces; set aside. (Note: Leave oven preheated to 325°F to bake tart.)

Toss the 2 cups of blueberries with the ¼ cup of sugar; set aside.

TO COMPLETE TART: Spread blueberry filling out evenly in the chilled tart shell.

Bake in preheated oven for 40 minutes, or until the tart shell is browned and crispy and the blueberries are fully cooked.

Press the blueberry and sugar topping gently onto the cooked tart. Sprinkle the crushed roasted hazelnuts over the top of the tart.

Cool before serving.

PEACH NAPOLEON

My version of the French dessert is made delectable by crisp layers of puff pastry combined with smooth creamy custard sauce. It can be topped with a light dusting of confectioners' sugar if desired.

WINE RECOMMENDATIONS:

CHATEAU STE. MICHELLE
Ethos Reserve Late Harvest White Riesling, Columbia Valley
OR
CHATEAU STE. MICHELLE
Late Harvest Chenin Blanc

FOR CRÈME ANGLAISE:

8 egg yolks

1 cup sugar

3 cups milk or half-and-half

½ teaspoon vanilla

FOR PEACHES:

3 cups peeled sliced peaches

½ cup Late Harvest Riesling

FOR DOUGH:

2 sheets frozen puff pastry dough, thawed

FOR SERVING:

1 cup whole fresh raspberries or sliced fresh strawberries

TO PREPARE CRÈME ANGLAISE: In a double boiler or heavy saucepan over medium-high heat, combine the egg yolks and sugar. Stir with a wooden spoon until thickened and smooth. Remove from heat.

In a separate saucepan, heat the milk or half-and-half to just boiling, being careful not to boil over. Remove the milk from heat. Return the egg mixture back to the stove on low heat and slowly add the heated milk, a little at a time, whisking constantly. Continue until all the milk is gone and the mixture has thickened, do not boil. Stir in the vanilla. Pass the mixture through a fine sieve. Chill.

TO PREPARE PEACHES: Marinate the peach slices in Late Harvest Riesling for 30 minutes.

TO PREPARE DOUGH: Preheat the oven to 350°F. Lay the pastry sheets on top of each other and cut the pastry dough into 8 triangles. Bake on a cookie sheet until brown, about 12 minutes. Set aside to cool.

TO SERVE: Pull apart the triangles into 2 pieces, top and bottom. Place 1 tablespoon of the crème Anglaise over the bottom portion of each triangle. Put ¼ of the peach filling on the triangle. Place the top portion of the triangle back on top. Pour 1 tablespoon of the crème Anglaise on top. Top with the raspberries or strawberries.

RASPBERRY PARFAIT

½ cup heavy cream

½ cup sour cream

1 cup fresh or frozen raspberries

Squeeze of lemon juice

2 tablespoons sugar

Mint sprigs, for garnish

Whole raspberries, for garnish

This dessert can be made in less than ten minutes and is perfect when there is little time for a complicated masterpiece.

Whip the heavy cream until stiff peaks form. Fold the whipped cream into the sour cream in a medium bowl. Stir in the lemon juice and sugar. Gently stir in the berries, reserving some as garnish.

Spoon the mixture into parfait glasses. Garnish with the mint sprigs and raspberries.

Ricotta Cheese and Berry "Parfait"

Sweet fresh berries are awakened with the flavor of balsamic vinegar, and buttery soft cheeses are enhanced with cocoa. The result satisfies even the chocolate lovers!

1 cup ricotta cheese

1 cup marscarpone

2 tablespoons powdered sugar

Pinch vanilla bean, finely chopped

Scant ⅛ teaspoon orange zest

1 tablespoons cocoa powder

2 cups mixed berries

1 tablespoon balsamic vinegar

Mint sprigs, for garnish

Beat the ricotta, mascarpone, sugar, vanilla bean, and orange zest with a mixer until smooth.

Place half the cheese mixture into another bowl. Mix in the cocoa powder until well combined.

Slice the berries and toss with the balsamic vinegar.

To assemble, spoon a small amount of the white cheese mixture into a parfait glass or martini glass. Top with the cocoa cheese mixture. Place a layer of the berries. Continue layering the white cheese, cocoa cheese, and berries until there are 3 layers and the glass is full. Garnish with mint.

Wine
Recommendation:

Chateau Ste. Michelle
*Ethos Reserve Late Harvest
White Riesling,
Columbia Valley*

SCHIACCIATA (FALL HARVEST GRAPE CAKE WITH FENNEL)

CHEF KIM WISS, ANTICA NAPA VALLEY

2 teaspoons dried yeast

8 ounces warm water

12 ounces flour

12 tablespoons superfine sugar, divided

7 tablespoons olive oil, divided

1 teaspoon salt

3 pounds seedless red grapes

½ cup concentrated grape juice

½ teaspoon fennel seed (or rosemary), chopped

1 egg, beaten

Place yeast in warm water and stir. Allow to ferment (bubble).

In a separate bowl, combine the flour, 4 tablespoons of sugar, 5 tablespoons of olive oil, and salt. Add yeast mixture; stir and fully mix. Allow to rise in warm place, covered, for about 1 hour.

Preheat the oven to 350°F.

Remove dough and divide into 4 portions. Roll out each portion to about ¼-inch thick.

Oil two 8-inch round nonstick cake pans. Place a layer of the dough in one pan and fit to the sides, allowing the dough to come up and over about ½ inch. Sprinkle with 2 tablespoons of sugar, 1½ teaspoons of olive oil, and half the fennel.

Place a layer of grapes on the dough. Include 3 tablespoons of the concentrated grape juice. The grapes should come up ½ of the way to the top of the cake pan.

Place another layer of dough on the grapes, and tuck into the side of the pan, press the dough down, so that your fingers outline the grapes within the cake. Place another layer of grapes on top, sprinkle with 2 tablespoons of sugar, and 1½ teaspoons of olive oil. Fold over the dough from the bottom layer, to make a partial cover of the grapes—it will fold over about 1 inch.

Brush additional olive oil over the folded over dough and a little directly on the grapes.

Repeat above to make second cake.

Bake in preheated oven for approximately 1 hour.

This cake is served all over Italy during the harvest season—August through October. At the winery, we use Sangiovese grapes, including the seeds, with freshly pressed juice to make this traditional cake.

For this recipe use the sweetest grapes you can find, if not add a little additional sugar. The cake tastes terrific warm and served with a dollop of fresh mascarpone, although that is not traditional.

WINE RECOMMENDATIONS:

ANTICA NAPA VALLEY
Chardonnay
OR
Cabernet Sauvignon

Sweet Ricotta Raisin Pudding

Sweet and spicy, creamy and delicious! Reminiscent of Italian comfort food— from the old country.

½ cup golden raisins
¼ cup cognac or rum
½ cup milk
1 cup white rice
1 cup ricotta cheese

¼ cup sugar
¼ teaspoon cinnamon
⅛ teaspoon mace
⅛ cup heavy cream

Soak the raisins in the cognac or rum for about 30 minutes.

Pour the milk to a medium-size saucepan with a lid. Add the rice and heat until just simmering (with the lid off). Turn heat to low; cover. Cook for 15 minutes, until the rice is very soft. Cool.

Stir together the raisins, cooked rice, ricotta, sugar, cinnamon, and mace until well mixed. If the pudding seems dry, moisten by adding 1 tablespoon of cream at a time until consistency is moist and creamy.

RECIPE INDEX